W9-BNH-221

DATE DUE

TEACHING THINKING AND LITERACY

Gary A. Negin
California State University

UNIVERSITY
PRESS OF
AMERICA

Lanham • New York • London

Copyright © 1992 by
University Press of America®, Inc.
4720 Boston Way
Lanham, Maryland 20706

3 Henrietta Street
London WC2E 8LU England

Library of Congress Cataloging-in-Publication Data
Negin, Gary A.
Teaching Thinking and Literacy / Gary A. Negin.
p.   cm.
Includes bibliographical references and index.
1. Thought and thinking—Study and teaching—United States.
2. English language—Study and teaching—United States.
3. Reading.   4. Study, Method of.   I. Title.
LB1590.3.N44   1991
428.4' 07—dc20   91-30511 CIP

ISBN 0-8191-8478-0 (cloth : alk. paper)
ISBN 0-8191-8479-9 (pbk. : alk. paper)

----------------------------------Table of Contents------------------------

Chapter 1: *The Challenge of Making Sense of the World*

Introduction	1
Generalization: Description	6
Hypothesis: Explanation	16
Evaluation: Judgement	21
Language and Thought	26
Conclusion	30

Chapter 2: The Reading Process

Introduction	31
Variables that Influence Reading	33
Variables Associated with the Reader	34
Variables Associated with the Text	41
Variables Associated with the Environment	44
A Description of the Reading Process	48
Conclusion	64

Chapter 3: The Writing Process

Introduction	65
Variables that Influence Writing	69
Variables Associated with the Author	69
Variables Associated with the Text	73
Variables Associated with the Audience	75
Variables Associated with the Environment	76
A Description of the Writing Process	79
Conclusion	85

Chapter 4: Study Strategies

Introduction	87
Flexible Reading Rates	90
Organizing and Recording Information	92
Retention	96
Preparing for Examinations	99
Conducting Research	105
In Libraries	105
Through Interviews	110
Time Management	111

Chapter 5: Making Decisions About Instruction

Introduction	113
Obtaining Diagnostic Information	115
Establishing Goals	116
Selecting Facilities and Materials	116
Choosing Procedures	121
Formulating a Measurement and Evaluation Plan	122
Teaching a Primary Generalization	124
Teaching a Hypothesis	127
Teaching an Evaluation	133
Conclusion	138
Index	139

Dedication

To Toad, Whazzat, and Boo-Boo

Introduction to Chapter #1

In the first sentence of <u>The Books of Bokonon</u>, Kurt Vonnegaut states, "All of the true things I am about to tell you are shameless lies."[1] He continues by explaining that he can only tell you his view of things, a view which may be different from others. We want to give you the same caution. We are going to lie to you.

---

[1]Kurt Vonnegut, <u>Cat's Cradle</u>, (New York: Delacorte Press, 1963), p. 16.

Chapter 1
The Challenge of Making Sense of the World

Wonder and Mystery. The things we want to know and the things we do not know. The desire to understand what we do not understand. The search for knowledge.

How do we know we know? How do we come to know? What is knowledge? These are the questions of epistemology, the study of the assumptions, procedures, and conclusions that lead to knowledge.

Skeptics criticize attempts to understand knowing by arguing that humans are incapable of knowing truth; of being absolutely and objectively certain. First, skeptics believe that there are no fundamental, unquestionable principles (a priori statements) for people to use as a foundation when they build knowledge. People cannot be certain that they exist, have bodies, control their thoughts, or are in contact with real, external objects. Perhaps, as Descartes suggested, we are dreaming our lives, or are being manipulated by an evil higher power to believe in baseless convictions.[2] Perhaps we are characters in someone else's dream, actors in an ethereal play. We assume things will be as they have been. Maybe, however, gravity will vanish and the baseball won't fall into the fielder's glove as we watch the play. Maybe the future will not resemble the past and present. Volumes of philosophical material have discussed the quest for certainty. While the issue is intellectually interesting, we will take the position that a priori statements are not necessary, since people can live even though their knowledge can be doubted. We only need to know that we believe something is. We agree with Maritain that the aim of epistemology is not so much to answer "Can we know?" but to discover the conditions under which we can know, and the extent and limits of our knowing.[3]

Second, skeptics believe that people are uniquely individual and fallible instruments who experience and construct their worlds imperfectly and indirectly for numerous reasons. First, the diamond we think we see is experienced fleetingly. If we consider a diamond to consist of atoms that continuously move in space, the diamond changes as we look at it and no diamond is ever the same

---

[2]Ralph M. Easton, ed., Descartes Selections, (New York: Scribners, 1927), pp. 90-95.

[3]Jacques Maritain, The Degree of Knowledge, trans. Gerold B. Phelan (New York: Scribners, 1959), p. 73.

from experience to experience. No two experiences, no matter how close in time, are exactly alike. Each sensory experience is separate in time, space, and quality. Second, our perspective may affect our understanding. For example, a round-cut diamond will look like a flat circle from directly overhead, and a cone from the side or underneath. The diamond will look large and faceted up-close, and small and smooth from a distance. Third, the type and quality of the instruments we use in our observations can affect what we see. The flaws in a diamond appear most clearly within a certain range of magnification under a microscope, a power that is greater than can be obtained from a low-powered magnifying glass that is intended as a reading aid. The flaws could not be seen even with the correct magnification, if the microscope's lenses were severely scratched. Fourth, the absence or presence of the observer may change the characteristics of the object. A diamond is warmer and lets less light pass through when held in a person's hand. Fifth, an unintentional bias may alter our interpretation of data. Our strong belief in the honesty of a friendly jeweler may make us discount the seriousness of the flaws in a diamond we examine. Sixth, environmental conditions may affect experience. For example, the amount of light in the room will help us determine the diamond's clarity and reflective quality. An absence of light would prevent us from seeing the diamond at all. Seventh, the diamond is experienced indirectly through our eyes, nerves, and minds. As a result, our understanding comes second-hand through a visual system whose physiological condition may adversely affect our understanding of an external world.

Most importantly, we rely on our memories to help us understand. Memory leads us to see what we think we are seeing. We create, remember, and use general categories to classify our experiences so we can add order and sense to our experiences. Meaning transcends the sensory data we receive about a particular diamond. Meaning comes from the categories which tell us how a diamond is different from topaz and glass.

What assurances do we have, however, to allow us to believe that our categories are correctly and fully formed? For example, some ancient people considered diamonds to be splinters from the stars, or crystallized lightning; so they thought they saw objects that came from the sky when they looked at diamonds. A lack of experience or correct interpretation may prevent memory from being accurate. We can't remember accurate information if something was never correctly understood. We can't remember something we never knew.

Memory of our constructed categories is vital, but not totally reliable, even when we have something valuable to remember. Memory is complicated, since there is no guarantee that we remember what we know correctly. Error in interpretation can be compounded due to retrieval error. A mind, like a computer, can misread an accurate file or misread an inaccurate file thereby making errors or making more errors. Memory is complicated because we can delude ourselves into remembering something that never happened, like describing events when we are drunk, or recalling an earlier reincarnation. Memory is complicated since it can be altered without our realization by new insights which enter our subconscious minds after our first memorable experience. Memory is complicated when we try to remember things that are out of our direct experience. We don't remember the Civil War. We remember reading or hearing about it from a source outside ourselves. It is further from us than an idea, event, or object we can experience in the present or remember from immediate data. The probability of error usually increases as we move away from direct experience.

The picture presented so far is bleak if we accept that nothing is known for certain, and that human limitations prevent us from knowing very well. Does this mean that humans are doomed to eternal ignorance and gloom? No. It may not be certain to believe that we really exist, that the future will be like the past, or that the world is organized and ordered; but it is practical to believe so. Our common experience tells us that we are pragmatic beings who seek to add meaning to our lives because the existential alternative is unpleasant. If we do not strive to become, to add more and more meaning to our lives, we will experience what Kierkegaard calls the "sickness unto death," the loneliness, meaninglessness, and nothingness that pervades our lives as we wait to die in a nonsensical world.[4] As the United States Army proclaims, it is important to be all you can be. We add order and meaning to survive life's perils. We do not have an acceptable alternative.

Let's examine the implications of our conclusion that we must live life to the best of our abilities. First, it must be noted that each of us must take responsibility for our own life. As astute as it sounds, if you don't do your part, it won't get done. We must make our own active, continuous search for knowledge. Our knowledge is an attempt to express our attachment to being and becoming. We aren't what we are; we become what we are. Unlike a diamond that will remain basically unchanged after its creation, perhaps with only a little cutting and polishing being added, people perpetually change. Our becoming is influenced by the future, as well as by our past. We cannot deny the effects of

---

[4]Soren Kierkegaard, The Sickness Unto Death, trans. Walter Lowrie (Princeton: Princeton University Press, 1941).

time and sensation.

Second, we should not conceive of information as true or false, fact or opinion, standard or creative. These are simplistic and confusing notions. We will take the position that all thought is creative, since every thought is a new thought. You are having a thought now. It wasn't in your mind a moment ago, even if it's a thought you or someone else had before. Every thought is also creative because it is the product of a unique mind. No thought can mean exactly the same thing to any two people, since the quantity, type, and quality of people's experiences vary. We will take the position that facts do not exist. Everything is an opinion, although some ideas are more verifiable than others. We will take the position that everything is false, but that some things are less false than others. As Fred Silverman, a former television program director, once said, "All television shows are trash, but some are better than others. There is bad trash and good trash." Ultimate truth cannot be known. Even if we met God (If God exists.), we could not understand him/her due to our human limitations. We could only understand pure truth if we were of a different nature.

Third, we will take the position that life moves so quickly that it is impossible for us to sample and sift data that would make us nearly certain of our decisions. We act when we have enough evidence; we do not wait for near-certitude. We take a chance. We gamble.

Fourth, there are a few broad categories that are convenient, powerful organizers which help us make sense of the world. In this chapter, we will modestly suggest that assertions about the world can be classified into three categories. Assertions can be generalizations, hypotheses, or evaluations. Briefly, generalizations help us <u>recognize</u> and <u>describe</u>. They answer questions such as, "What? Where? When? How many?" Hypotheses <u>explain</u>. They answer the question "Why?" Evaluations <u>judge</u>. They answer the question "What good?"

Generalization: Description

An assertion is a declarative statement that notes a meaningful relationship between ideas. Greetings, commands, and questions are not assertions, since they do not denote relationships. Assertions can be used to express generalizations. A generalization implies that members of a group invariably have common characteristics. If we ask, "What is a diamond?" the answer could be the generalization, "A diamond is a transparent precious stone of pure carbon in crystallized form; the hardest substance known." From our various sensory and intellectual experiences with diamonds, we separated characteristics found in all diamonds from characteristics that differed in individual diamonds. In other words, we generalized. After examining instances of diamonds, we defined, or categorized, diamonds based on the similarities that we considered basic. We developed an abstract idea that helped us understand, organize, and simplify the enormous amount of sensory data we received. We went beyond particular experiences and inferred that they could all be classified as members of the same group. A generalization concerns class inclusion.

A single definition of a word in a dictionary is a primary generalization; a statement that objects or thoughts with certain characteristics are similar enough to be placed in the same category. A definition should state necessary and sufficient conditions. What is a diamond? It is basic (necessary) that a diamond be a stone, but more information is needed to categorize a stone as a diamond. Other necessary criteria are that the stone be transparent and precious. Still, other objects can be categorized as transparent, precious stones. We must add (pure carbon, crystallized form, hardest substance known) to our definition so that we can adequately (sufficiently) describe a diamond. We must have enough important information so our category of diamond does not include objects that aren't diamonds.

Ideal definitions that list all necessary attributes are hard to create or find, so we must often settle for adequate definitions. Adequate definitions satisfy our immediate needs, but aren't complete enough to help us categorize in all circumstances we might encounter. For example, it is easy for us to consider our neighbor's vehicle with four wheels and a gas-combustible engine to be an automobile. Our definition of an automobile in this case is based on some, but not all of the characteristics, that would be included in an ideal definition. Our definition may satisfy our current needs, but it would not be sufficient if we were to encounter an unfamiliar vehicle with three wheels and an engine powered by batteries. Should this new object be considered to be an automobile?

Our need for an ideal definition depends, in part, on the consequences of being wrong. Better definitions are needed whenever we want to increase the likelihood of being right. We want to be thorough when the risk of being wrong is great. What would happen if we refused to call this new vehicle an automobile? Nothing? If so, we needn't worry about an ideal definition, since a poor definition would work almost as well. A great deal? If we did not want to risk a low grade in class, a loss of a wager, or a punch in the nose from an offended neighbor, we would want to consider carefully an ideal definition before deciding what to call the vehicle in question.

The quality of a definition also depends on whether we need to recognize or describe an object or idea. We may not need an ideal definition to help us recognize, as much as we would if we were asked to describe. In the first instance we need only a shallow understanding; in the second we need a deeper understanding. For example, we would not need to know a comprehensive definition of book if we could locate the desired object when someone referred to it as a libro. All we would need to know is that the two terms refer to the same object. Translation would be enough. We would not need to have an ideal definition of aquanaut, if we knew that it was derived from the latin words aqua and nautilos meaning water and sailor. An etymological definition would be enough. We would not need to have an ideal definition of hilarious, if we knew it meant about the same thing as funny. A synonymous definition would be enough to relate an unfamiliar term to a familiar one. Nominal definitions (translation, etymological, synonymous) suffice when the basic meaning of a term is already understood.

The difference between recognition and description is familiar to college students. Think about two types of tests that you are used to taking: multiple-choice and essay tests. It is easier for you to be successful on a multiple-choice test than on an essay test when your understanding is limited. You only have to have your memory jogged by a stimulus on the multiple-choice test, and you have the assurance that the correct answer is already on paper. When you take an essay test, the pages in front of you are blank. You must create a comprehensive and correct answer. As a result, you need a deeper understanding of the information in order to be successful.

If we were to describe something that is unfamiliar to another person, we would have to go beyond nominal definitions. Our definitions would have to approach the ideal. How do we know how much detail must be included in our definitions? The answer depends on the background knowledge of the person we are addressing and on the context in which the information is presented. When the audience is knowledgeable about related ideas, description is easier than when the audience knows little relevant information. One approach to definition that moves beyond nominal definitions is to describe through properties. This type of definition is called distinctive definition. We could use a distinctive definition when we tell our audience about the key feature(s) of the object or idea in question. It may be enough to tell our audience that a diamond is the hardest substance known, since that single characteristic separates diamonds from all other objects. We could use a genetic definition to describe. A genetic definition describes by telling how something originates. For example, chemical compounds are defined in this way. Carbon dioxide consists of one part of carbon and two parts of oxygen. A diamond can be genetically defined by referring to it as crystallized carbon. We could use a causal definition to describe. One type of causal definition identifies the producer(s) of an object and another type identifies the purpose(s). It may be enough to say that Jonas Salk created a vaccine for poliomyelitis. It may be enough to say that extreme pressure makes diamonds. It might be enough to tell an audience that a refrigerator cools food. It might be enough to tell an audience that diamonds can be used to scratch or cut softer substances. Finally, the various types of definition can be used in combination. The type(s) of definition and the specific detail provided depends on the interests and knowledge of the audience. Good instruction requires that teachers be able to switch to alternative descriptions when students fail to understand.

As indicated above, the type and amount of detail in our definitions depends on the background knowledge of our audience. In addition, the type and amount of detail in our definitions depends on the context in which the information is presented. If a diamond were shown to a class, without any other stone being present, very little information would be needed for students to know which object was the diamond. The teacher might use an accidental definition. An accidental definition describes by noting attributes. For example, the teacher may say that the transparent stone that is in the display case is a diamond. It is not sufficient to describe a diamond as a transparent stone. It is not an ideal definition that satisfies necessary and sufficient conditions, but it may be adequate for the circumstances, since students do not have to contrast the diamond with any other transparent stone in the room. More information would have to be given, however, if a precious diamond had to be contrasted with a baseball diamond. Yet, since there is a great deal of difference between a precious stone and a baseball infield, students would not need much information to be able to distinguish between the two objects. The most information would have to be given in a third case, if a diamond were presented alongside an emerald. In this case, the diamond would no longer be the only transparent stone in the room. Information would be needed so students could distinguish between the diamond and the emerald. Perhaps the teacher could describe the emerald as being a green transparent stone and the diamond as a clear transparent stone. This would not be an ideal definition for emerald or diamond, but would be enough of a definition for students to contrast two similar objects.

Two other special types of generalization need to be mentioned: functional generalizations and statistical generalizations. A functional generalization means that a change in one variable is closely related to a change in another variable. The statement, "Diamond finds vary with the level of mining activity," is a functional generalization. We can describe the relationship between diamond finds and mining activity by saying, for example, that miners usually find more diamonds when they are active than when they are inactive. A statistical generalization refers to a result stated as a ratio, percentage, or proportion. A statistical generalization refers to the frequency of a characteristic in a population. The statement, "More men than women die before seventy years of age," is a statistical generalization.

Generalization is a broader category than hypothesis or evaluation. As a result, we generalize more often than we hypothesize or evaluate. Generalizations help us answer common questions such as, "What? Where? When? How many?" Generalizations can describe the world of objects, thoughts, and events. A generalization can describe a concept, such as diamond. A generalization can describe a process or procedure, such as the steps in the manufacture of artificial diamonds. A generalization can describe relationships among variables, such as in the statement, "The degree of crystallization within a chunk of carbon depends on the pressure that was applied." A generalization can describe a statistical characteristic, as is, "Fifty-one percent of the babies born each year in the United States are male."

___Table 1_____

The following items are examples of generalizations. Note that each item describes. It is not necessary to know which specific type of generalization is illustrated.

English

1.   A play is a public theatrical exhibition.
2.   An author develops ideas, writes a first draft, revises the manuscript, then carefully transcribes the work so it makes a good impression on the audience.
3.   Poor spellers tend to be poor readers.
4.   The average household in Austin, Texas spends more on books each year than the average household in the United States by a margin of 3.43:1.

Social Studies

1.   A hermit opts for isolation over social interaction.
2.   Historians examine primary sources such as artifacts, before examining

Table 1, **continued**

secondary sources such as reports written by other historians who did not directly experience an event.

3.   The burden of proof increases in relation to the severity of the crime.
4.   Approximately 480 people are born every two minutes.

Mathematics

1.   A straight line is a long narrow mark, either straight or curved, traced on a surface.
2.   Algebraic logic requires that multiplication and division be carried out before addition and subtraction in a series of operations.
3.   distance=rate x time
4.   The front of a coin will appear approximately 50 percent of the time after a fair coin is flipped into the air and allowed to land without interference.

Natural Sciences

1.   Cobalt 60 is a radioactive isotope of cobalt with mass number 60 and exceptionally intense gamma ray activity.
2.   Electronics technicians inspect, repair, then test equipment.
3.   Cold-blooded animals have body temperatures that vary with the external environment.
4.   Paper products outnumber plastic products in American landfills by a ratio of 4:1.

Fine Arts

1.   "Everything you can imagine is real."   Pablo Picasso
2.   A clay pot is formed and glazed before being heated in a kiln.
3.   Paintings tend to increase in value after their creators die.
4.   Almost all professional jazz trumpeters are men.

Mechanical Arts

1.   A plane is a carpenter's tool with an adjustable blade for smoothing and leveling wood.
2.   When drilling a screw hole in wood, a drill bit that is smaller than the diameter of the screw is used first, then a bit of equal diameter is used to redrill the first two-thirds of the hole, then a countersink bit is used to

Table 1, continued

     reshape the top of the hole.
3.   Harder metals are more difficult to bend.
4.   More plywood than mahogany is used in the construction of houses.

     How do we form generalizations? Generalizations result when we create meaning that transcends experience; when we intellectually order and organize what has happened to us. All of our experiences contribute to understanding: planned and unplanned. We draw a particular type of conclusion (generalization) from the data we gathered, and assert it verbally when we want to communicate it to ourselves or others. In other words, a generalization is a type of conclusion based on evidence that can be expressed with a verbal assertion. Individuals, however, can hold generalizations in mind without being aware of them. A person can have thoughts that have never been verbalized. As you will see later in this chapter, thinking can occur without conscious awareness or language.

     Let's examine an example of generalization formation. The first time you tasted coffee, you may have confused it with something you knew. You may have thought it was spoiled cocoa, or a different type of cocoa than you had experienced. It is natural to expect things to be familiar. Such an attitude prevents us from feeling overwhelmed. It may even be possible that your misconception of coffee as a type of cocoa never had to be changed, if no practical, unfortunate consequences resulted. Your description of coffee was not in agreement with most other people's, but maybe it didn't matter to you or them, or no one knew of the discrepancy. A second alternative was for you to decide that you tasted something that was so distinctive that you had to create a new category to describe it. You came to the conclusion that liquids that tasted this way should be considered as being different from cocoa. Next, you may have attached a label or term to your category, although this was not necessary, and the term could have been any one you wanted. For example, you may have decided to call the liquid, "mudruck." When language is discussed later in this chapter, we will deal again with this issue of the subjective and conventional assignment of terms to referents. Finally, additional experiences with coffee, similar drinks, and very different drinks may lead you to change your conclusion whether you believed coffee was spoiled cocoa, a different type of cocoa, or a distinctive entity. Even if you believe you are dealing with a unique liquid, your generalization (category, definition, description) will be refined as you learn more about varieties of coffee plants, growing and harvesting procedures, processing, preparation, and the particular tastes of the varieties.   Your generalization will also be improved as you experience other drinks.   You will learn by comparing and contrasting; by deciding how things are alike and, most importantly, how they are different.

The number of possible experiences that you could have with coffee and all other drinks is enormous.   You could never experience everything you would need to know to approach complete familiarity.   You sample from the universe of potential experiences.   It was stated earlier in this chapter that people gather and sift evidence as they consider the consequence of being wrong, until they feel confident to act.   Two other variables determine the quantity of data which we gather: time and cost.   Sometimes we have to act when others force us.   The time we are given to make a decision is constrained.   If a car is driving straight at us on the highway, we cannot take the time to consider the generalization that, "Cars moving straight towards each other tend to collide."   Sometimes we have the luxury of waiting until we think it is expedient to act.   We do not have to grab the first bag of cookies that we see on the shelves at the grocery store and hope that it contains chocolate-chip cookies.   We can shop leisurely, carefully reading the names and ingredients printed on bags until we are confident that we have identified a bag of chocolate-chip cookies to purchase.   Of course, we like other kinds of cookies just as well, and would happily eat whatever kind we had blindly picked.   The consequence of an incorrect choice isn't really a concern.   We are simply taking advantage of the time we have to choose exactly what we want. The cost of gathering evidence before making a generalization may be prohibitive.   For example, we may wish to become wine connoisseurs, but can't afford to buy hundreds of bottles, travel to distant locations, or recuperate from frequent hangovers before confidently describing the typical taste of even one variety of wine.

We have seen that the quantity of evidence we need before making a generalization depends on the consequence of being wrong, on the time we have to draw the conclusion, and on the cost of gathering data.   Another concern, the quality of the evidence that we gather, has also been discussed.   Remember that human limitations and mechanical limitations of the instruments we use prevent us from knowing very well.   It was also mentioned that we often believe the generalizations offered by authorities, especially when we are separated from directly experiencing important objects, ideas, and events because of time or place.   Since students rely extensively on the conclusions of authorities, such as textbook authors and teachers, special attention needs to be paid to the evaluation of authoritative sources.   Six criteria should be applied when considering the credibility of an authority. First, the expertise of the authority must be in the field at issue. Second, no conflict of interest should be apparent. The authority should not have a financial or emotional interest at stake that would jeopardize objectivity. Third, the authority should be respected by professional colleagues. Fourth, other respected authorities should corroborate the information. Fifth, appropriate instruments, such as microscopes and telescopes, should be used for observing. Sixth, established procedures should be followed when collecting evidence.

The need for established procedures is well known to adherents of the scientific method. Scientists examine a phenomenon, develop a prediction for testing, establish conditions for an experiment, conduct the experiment, measure results, and evaluate results. This method is the standard problem solving technique that people often use to make decisions. For example, teachers follow this format when they develop lesson plans. Teachers diagnose a problem, establish a goal; choose appropriate facilities, materials, techniques, and deadlines; implement instruction, then measure and evaluate. As you will see in chapter #2, we will describe reading as a decision making process which follows the same steps whether the generalizations that are tested are letters or letter clusters, sound-symbol correspondences, words, terms, phrases, ideas, passage structure, or other aspects of reading. The standard problem solving technique is also used to regulate thinking, as in the concept of metacognition which also will be described in chapter #2.

A final issue needs to be addressed in our discussion of generalizations. The issue follows nicely from our discussion of the scientific approach that scientists, other researchers, and learners use. We need to describe sampling techniques, which help us reduce the time for and costs of collecting evidence, and improve the quality of the evidence we gather. It is beyond the scope of this chapter to describe the details of the sampling techniques that researchers employ, but we will mention a few key ideas. First, researchers (active learners) must carefully define the universe of relevant data from which they could sample to gather evidence that they will use to support a generalization (conclusion). For example, a social scientist may wish to determine which candidate will win the presidency before the election is held. The universe of relevant data would include the opinion of every citizen who would be qualified to vote on election day. The universe of relevant data would go beyond the opinion of a single qualified voter, and the opinions of the scientist's ten closest friends.

Second, a sampling technique must be selected. Since it is impractical to get everyone's opinion, the social scientist cannot achieve enumeration. That is, the scientist cannot collect every piece of relevant evidence. As a result, the scientist must sample a portion from the universe of opinion. To do this, the scientist may choose to take a true random sample, with each opinion having an equal and independent chance of being selected. In other words, it would be just as likely for your opinion to be asked as mine. This technique reduces potential bias, since scientists believe in probability, the assumption that the majority opinion would be closer to the truth than infrequently expressed opinions. The most frequently mentioned opinion should reflect the mood of the qualified voters. The most frequent answer should be representative. The scientist may choose to select a stratified random sample. This method further eliminates the likelihood of bias by identifying relevant layers (strata) in the universe and selecting a random sample from each layer in proportion to the number of instances in each layer. For example, a social scientist may believe that opinion may be a function of geographical location. Based on the origin of the candidates, the scientist suspects that people who live west of the Mississippi River will tend to vote differently from people who live east of the Mississippi River. As a result, the scientist may solicit opinions from 75 percent of the qualified voters in the west, and from 75 percent of the qualified voters in the east. Both areas would be equally represented. If a true random sample were used, it is possible that the scientist's sample would contain a disproportionate number of people from one of the two major areas, thereby biasing the results. The scientist may choose to take time-lapse samples. This third method of sampling reduces potential bias by recognizing that data may change over time. For example, a social scientist may realize that some qualified voters change their opinions often and sometimes for the slightest reasons. The results from a sample of opinion taken in July may be very different from results obtained from the same people at the beginning of November. The scientist would have even less confidence in the reliability of the results if the two samples involved different people.

Third, researchers must be concerned with the size of the sample selected. Confidence in generalizations (conclusions) increases as enumeration is approached. Social scientists are on firmer ground if they base their conclusions on a proportionately large sample, than on a proportionately small sample. A prediction about the outcome of a presidential election based on the opinions of one thousand qualified voters would not be as reliable as a prediction based on the opinions of one million qualified voters. How large should a sample be? Do we reach a point where our confidence in a generalization is not significantly increased if we add to our sample?

Fourth, researchers must decide how many samples they will take at a given time. One sample of the opinions of ten thousand people could be taken on the first day of November. It would be better, however, if 2, 20, 200, or 2,000 samples of the opinions of groups of ten thousand people were taken and the same result were obtained. This would increase confidence in the argument from instances which proves all types of generalizations: "If all known instances are the same, then all new instances will be the same." Confidence that the result is typical is increased as enumeration is approached. How many samples should be taken at the same time?

The important questions posed at the end of the last two paragraphs are answered in detail in textbooks on research methodology. Our brief answer is another question: "What is it worth to have confidence in your conclusion?" As we mentioned earlier, you can only decide after you consider the cost of collecting relevant evidence, the time given to make a decision, and the consequences of being wrong.

Hypothesis: Explanation

A generalization is a conclusion which accounts for a group of similar evidence. A generalization describes what something is. In contrast, a hypothesis is a conclusion that accounts for a group of different, relevant evidence. A hypothesis and its evidence explain why something is. Arguments which support hypotheses help us explain the past and predict the future.

Let's examine a hypothesis which explains how dinosaurs became extinct. The hypothesis (conclusion) is that dinosaurs died because a giant asteroid collided with the earth. This conclusion seems to account for different, relevant evidence. First, scientists believe that a collision with an asteroid could have sent a large cloud of dust or water vapor into the air, initially blocking out the sun's rays and cooling the planet. Eventually, however, the dust and water could have created a greenhouse effect that would have sent global temperatures soaring. Second, an asteroid would create huge amounts of carbon dioxide, a greenhouse gas, if it hit carbonate rock such as limestone. Third, a fine layer of an element rare on earth, but found in abundance in asteroids, has been discovered in numerous sites around the world. Fourth, sophisticated dating techniques indicate that the rare element was deposited on the earth's surface about 65 million years ago. Fifth, a recent study of changes in the shape of the leaves of fossilized plants from 65 million years ago indicates a precipitous drop in temperature for one to two months followed by a fourfold increase in rainfall and an 18 degree Fahrenheit rise in temperature over the next 500,000 to one million years. Sixth, the climatic changes occurred at precisely the time that the dinosaurs disappeared from the face of the earth. The six different pieces of evidence seem to converge upon the conclusion. We infer the conclusion from the evidence. We could summarize the argument, the evidence and the conclusion, by saying, "If an asteroid created a greenhouse effect, the greenhouse effect was intensified by carbon dioxide, a rare element from asteroids has been found on earth, the rare element was deposited 65 million years ago, leaves from fossilized plants from 65 million years ago indicate a precipitous drop in temperature, and the drastic climatic changes occurred at precisely the same time that dinosaurs disappeared from earth, then dinosaurs died because a giant asteroid collided with the earth."

The argument that was just presented can be criticized since it is a probable argument. Scientists can never be certain. The evidence and the hypothesis can be challenged. Scientists are only guessing when they say that an asteroid caused the dinosaurs to die. Evidence can be challenged on the basis of validity, reliability, relevancy, probability, and sufficiency. For example, scientists can't be certain that a single, huge asteroid ever collided with earth. As it stands, scientists have not been able to pinpoint precisely where the asteroid might have hit. Second, the margin of error for dating techniques is enormous. Estimates on the ages of the fossils and the space dust could easily be unreliable. Third, it may be irrelevant that an element found in abundance in asteroids has been found in numerous places on earth. The element may naturally be found on earth, although it is uncommon. Also, the dust may not have been distributed after a collision with an asteroid. The elemental dust may have filtered down through the atmosphere like so much cosmic lint. Fourth, scientists are on very shaky ground when they estimate the probabilities of a huge asteroid hitting earth, of the collision causing a large and long-lasting blockage of the sun, and of the asteroid causing high levels of carbon dioxide after striking carbonate rock. The chance of any of these things happening is very slight, and the chance that they all happened together is astronomical. Fifth, the total weight of the evidence is not sufficient to convince beyond doubt that the explanation is correct, even if we are impressed with the evidence. It may be plausible, but questions remain. Additional, relevant evidence would enhance the argument. Was the entire earth blocked by the sun? Would dinosaurs be dramatically affected by a mere 18 degree change in temperature over 500,000 to one million years? Did the temperature change to the same extent (when decreasing or increasing) in every corner of the planet? Would a blockage of only two months have such a disastrous effect?

Finally, the hypothesis can be challenged. Alternative, plausible hypotheses can be created. When we try to understand the relationships among various evidence, it is best for us to consider as many plausible, alternative hypotheses as possible to increase the chances of our identifying the best one. Perhaps a catastrophic change in the climate occurred that was caused by forces that were unrelated to an asteroid. Perhaps an environmental change, in addition to a climate change, occurred that killed the dinosaurs. They might not have adapted to the change in time. Maybe the dinosaurs were infected by a contagious bacteria or virus. Perhaps dinosaurs maladapted as they evolved. Perhaps a space ship from the planet Zyzyx carried off the healthy dinosaurs to supply their barbecue restaurants and let the rest die! The possibility of an alien invasion should not be overlooked, as implausible as it may seem to you. A bias should not prevent you from exploring all possibilities and finding the best explanation.

Special attention needs to be paid to hypotheses regarding causal relationships, since an understanding of causality gives us control over environments. However, it is not simple to determine causality. In fact, it is difficult to define cause. There is no single definition of cause that conforms to all of the different uses of the word. We define <u>cause</u> as "the set of necessary and sufficient conditions of an event." Cause means that the necessary (basic, important) conditions and the sufficient condition (adequacy of the total) for the occurrence of an event are met. Certain antecedents must precede a particular consequent. Poliomyelitis is a virus that can cause paralysis in a person's body, but only if enough of it is present. In other words, it is necessary for the virus to be present in a body, but not sufficient. A particular amount is needed before a pathological result occurs. A smaller quantity may even prove to be helpful. Consider vaccines, such as the polio vaccine. Vaccines are small injections of toxic substances that can be problematic if given in larger doses. The body ultimately benefits, however, from a small dose as it builds immunity to the toxic substance.

Fortunately, a famous philosopher named John Stuart Mill described three ways of supporting hypotheses of causality: by agreement, difference, and variation.[5] The hypothesis (conclusion), "Microbes cause fermentation in beer," can be supported by agreement if at least two identical cases are examined which yield the same result; fermentation occurs in beer when microbes are added to mash. The supposed cause must always be present when the effect occurs. A hypothesis is strengthened as successful replications increase. Of course, it is not always easy for a researcher to identify the suspected cause of an effect. Many phenomena precede an effect. For example, the mash may be blessed by a

---

[5]John Stuart Mill, <u>A System of Logic</u>, (London: Longmans, Green and Company, 1884)).

religious person, mixed in a certain kettle, or prepared only on Tuesdays. A researcher (active learner) is faced with the problems of identifying the numerous phenomena, eliminating some of the phenomena from consideration, and proving which phenomenon causes another.

The hypothesis, "Microbes cause fermentation in beer," can also be supported by noting differences. This approach requires that the supposed cause must always be absent when the phenomenon fails to occur. We support the conclusion when we find that mash does not turn into beer without microbes. At least two cases must be examined for this approach to yield credibility. In one case, microbes must be added to the mash and fermentation must occur. In the second case, microbes must be absent and fermentation cannot occur. These two cases differ in respect to the presence or absence of the cause.

The method of difference is the most rigorous, but it demands complete control over all the variables in a situation, and is especially difficult to apply outside the natural sciences. Conditions must be exactly alike, except for the presence or absence of a single variable. The last approach to supporting the hypothesis that "Microbes cause fermentation in beer" is to note how a variation in the supposed cause changes the effect. For example, will the addition of a small amount of microbes cause the same change in a vat of mash as larger amounts?

We defined cause in the ideal sense of the term, when necessary and sufficient conditions are understood. In practice, scientists (researchers, active learners) are often satisfied when they know either the necessary or sufficient conditions. Practical considerations are involved. If scientists wish to produce something; such as a cure for a disease, synthetic rubber, or a stimulus to business activity, they need only know the sufficient conditions of these effects. If they wish to prevent or eliminate an effect, such as a disease, it is enough if they know the necessary conditions without which the disease cannot occur.

___Table 2_____

Each of the following items is an argument which includes a hypothesis and supportive evidence. Note that each item explains.

English

1.   Many of Herman Melville's stories contain a dark mood due to the

Table 2, **continued**

author's brooding and pessimistic nature.

2.   A recently discovered poem was attributed to Shakespeare since a statistical analysis of the vocabulary revealed that the poem contained approximately the predicted number of words that Shakespeare had not used before and words he used only once before, and the results were more dissimilar when compared to the expectations held for the works of Marlowe, Johnson, and Donne.

Social Studies

1.   If teenagers seek another place to belong due to a poor home life, pursue fantasy games, pursue religions, and pursue heavy metal music, then they will be drawn to satanism.

2.   President Franklin Roosevelt knew of the impending attack on Pearl Harbor, since the United States knew Japan's communication codes, a message had been intercepted noting Japan's plans, and visual contact was made with the Japanese fleet as it steamed toward Pearl Harbor.

Mathematics

1.   A navigator needs to have mathematical abilities, since navigation depends on solving problems of triangulation, and problems involving distance, rate, and time.

2.   Slide rules were replaced by electronic calculators since calculators were faster, more precise, computed more functions, and were less expensive.

Natural Sciences

1.   Since carbon is the smallest known atom, each carbon atom possesses four chemical bonds (the maximum possible), and the isometric geometrical pattern in diamonds compresses more chemical bonds into a given volume than any other substance; diamonds are the hardest substance known.

2.   People usually gain weight when they quit cigarette smoking because they eat more, eat more foods with sugar, and have slower rates of metabolism due to a decrease in nicotine.

Fine Arts

1.   Castrato singers were popular between the 16th and 18th centuries because

Table 2, continued

of their unique voices, powerful lungs, rigorous training, and because women were forbidden by St. Augustine to sing in Catholic churches.

2. Art Nouveau defied a lucid and encompassing definition, partly because it extended beyond the realm of the graphic, partly because the style underwent a metamorphosis during its brief span of life, and partly because its interpretation varied from country to country and often from artist to artist.

Mechanical Arts

1. Metal is easier to bend when heated, since expansion reduces density.
2. Plywood forced against a power sander will burn due to friction, and the flammability of the wood.

You may have noticed that some of the items in table 2 listed the evidence before the conclusion, and that the conclusion was stated before the evidence in others. Either way is acceptable.

You may have also wondered why the hypotheses were not listed by themselves, but rather in combination with the evidence they supported. The reason is because it is easy to confuse generalizations and hypotheses. The statement "Plywood forced against a power sander will burn." could be a generalization if it accounted for numerous occasions when plywood was forced against a sander, or it could be a hypothesis if it explained evidence gathered from various events or states of affairs, such as in the example in table 2.

Evaluation: Judgement

An evaluation states that something has or does not have value. Albert Einstein's comment, "Imagination is more important than information," is an example of an evaluation. An evaluation reflects an appraisal, a choice from among values. As appraisals, evaluations do not denote properties like size, color, weight, or hardness that can be verified. Properties such as these belong to an object, while values are located in the mind of an individual. Since values are extremely idiosyncratic, the strict criteria of empiricism and objectivity, which are used in the establishment of generalizations and hypotheses, are not applicable to values.

Generalizations, hypotheses, and evaluations are products of our efforts to make sense of the world. Generalizations and hypotheses give us a basic understanding. Evaluations add significance to our lives. Through evaluations, we separate worth from worthlessness. Through evaluations, we weigh our fundamental interactions with reality. We look at our relationship with ourselves, our relationship with the physical environment, our relationships with others, and our relationship with some transcendental power; and determine whether life is worth living.

How do we form evaluations? We form them as we interact with ourselves, objects, events, ideas, and others as we strive to find reward rather than punishment. As infants, we cried when our stomachs were empty or when our diapers were full in the hope that someone would feed us or change our clothes. We chose to seek reward over punishment. As we got older, we continued to learn behaviors and attitudes that would lead to reward. Sometimes values were foisted upon us. We may not have known alternative choices, or may not have had the power to choose a second alternative. As empowered adults, however, we are freer to be persuaded through reason, inspired by emotion, and motivated by a desire to emulate an exemplary model. We are in a better position, to recognize, create, and choose values for ourselves.

What values should we choose? We should choose the values that help us lead a righteous life. A righteous life is meaningful and admirable. A righteous person judges the comparative worth of evaluations by applying the traditional standards of <u>truth</u>, <u>beauty</u>, and <u>justice</u>. These standards provide reasons for claiming that a belief, object, or behavior is valuable.

An evaluation, like a generalization or hypothesis, is true (to the extent we can know) if it is in accordance with the evidence. In comparing two hypotheses, such as the theories of evolution and creation, people choose to prefer the one that best accounts for the evidence. The theory we choose as best should have more evidential consistency. The best theory has more value, because it gives us a better understanding of what we think is true. A second type of truth is personal truth. People should be true to their tastes; to what they hold dear. Our thoughts and actions should be consistent with our images of ourselves. We can believe in personal virtues such as freedom, sincerity, courage, liberty, moderation, financial security, emotional security, safety, health, and happiness.

Beauty is another standard that is used to form and weigh evaluations.

Virtues associated with aesthetic beauty include charm, loveliness, grandeur, harmony, symmetry, elegance, originality, and delicateness. A person may consider Michelangelo's statue of David to be beautiful because it is carefully crafted, proportional, symmetrical, and detailed. These are some of the qualities that are associated with sculptural beauty.

Justice is another important standard which can be applied when evaluations are formed and appraised. Justice can be found in social and religious realms. In the social realm, people may believe that it is worthy to try to do what is best for a community. In American society, individual initiative and equality are highly valued, yet the desires of individuals must be occasionally abrogated for the benefit of others. For example, a person may wish to kill others, but society punishes such behavior by law for the greater good of the community. There are winners and losers when evaluations conflict. Other social virtues include fairness, cooperation, charity, honesty, love, and trust. In the religious realm, people prefer to think and act in harmony with their concept of a transcendental power. A transcendental power is a superhuman power that is given credit for creating and governing the universe. Of course, atheists would eliminate this category from consideration. It is beyond the scope of this text, and the knowledge of the authors, to argue the relative merits of conceptualizations of transcendental power. It is important, however, to note that evaluations can be formed and appraised by examining their consistency with a particular religious philosophy. For example, a decision to act mercifully would be in accordance with Judeo-Christian tradition.

Although an evaluation can be formed on the basis of a single standard, most evaluations are formed because they appeal to two or more of the evaluative standards. For example, Mr. Johnston placed his grandfather clock in the corner of his living room, because it suited his taste. The placement seemed appropriate because his family had traditionally placed grandfather clocks in their living rooms. In addition, Mr. Johnston felt that the clock visually balanced the room. Its width, height, style, and color complemented the other furniture. Finally, Mr. Johnston felt that visitors, as well as family members, would benefit since the clock would be in a public room that was frequently used to entertain guests. The placement of the clock, therefore, was determined by an evaluation based on personal truth, aesthetic beauty, and social justice.

Evaluations are supported through arguments based on reason. There is no criterion, however, that can be used to accept or reject an evaluation with the convincing force that objectivity gives to an argument supporting a generalization or hypothesis. The evidence from the external world that would be relevant in supporting a generalization (numerous invariable cases) or a hypothesis (a variety of evidence accounted for) would be irrelevant in the case of an evaluation since the first piece of evidence in an argument supporting an evaluation is another personal appraisal, another evaluation. This appraisal has to be accepted by the audience in order for the argument to continue. If the audience rejects the appraisal, the argument cannot continue. The arguer and the audience have agreed to disagree.

Let's look at an example of an argument that supports an evaluation. How could we convince someone else of the evaluation (conclusion), "Ralph Nader is a good person."? First, we have to describe the characteristic(s) of a good person that we think is (are) important in this case. We might say that "All people who are concerned about consumers are good." Note that this is an evaluation. If the audience will not accept our evaluation, we cannot continue to support our point. The argument cannot be made. If the audience accepts our evaluation, we continue by supporting the hypothesis, "Ralph Nader is concerned about consumers." We might convince the audience by arguing that, "Since Ralph Nader established a nonprofit organization to benefit consumers, writes pamphlets that describe consumer rights, and publishes research reports that inform consumers of dangerous products; then Ralph Nader is concerned about consumers." Now we can present the entire argument, "If all people who are concerned about consumers are good, and Ralph Nader is concerned about consumers; then Ralph Nader is good." This argument is called an argument from convenience, since the discussants find it helpful to accept a prerequisite evaluation. The argument takes the general form, "If this prerequisite evaluation is accepted, and this hypothesis is supported; then the evaluation in question is acceptable."

Notice that the argument begins on shaky ground, since it can start with any evaluation. That is why arguments which support evaluations are not as compelling as those which support generalizations or hypotheses. The prerequisite evaluation could be repulsive, no matter how many people agree to accept it. People are not infallible. Humans are not perfect. We make mistakes. If we accept the evaluation "Anyone who kills rabbits is good," we could argue that, "Since anyone who kills rabbits is good, and Joe kills rabbits; then Joe is good."

___Table 3_____

Each of the following items is an evaluation. Remember that an evaluation judges. An evaluation declares value by answering, "What good is it?" Note that

Table 3, **continued**

the items are evaluations, whether you agree with the conclusions or not.

English

1.   William Shakespeare was a great poet.
2.   A poem that has a consistent rhyming scheme is better than a poem that doesn't use rhyme.

Social Studies

1.   Lyndon Johnson contributed greatly to the advancement of civil rights.
2.   Chinese Emperor Chin Shih Huang (221-210 B.C.) was right when he burned all books, except those about agriculture, astronomy, and medicine.

Mathematics

1.   The metric system is the best system of measurement.
2.   College students who are preparing to be elementary school teachers should not study trigonometry.

Natural Sciences

1.   It is better to use animals in preliminary medical experiments, than to use people.
2.   Poison gases should be used in warfare.

Fine Arts

1.   Art is only good if it appeals to a majority of people in a society.
2.   The cubist movement was an abomination of art.

Mechanical Arts

1.   Birds-eye maple wood is prettier than sugar maple wood.
2.   Mechanical pencils are better than wood pencils when drafting.

Philosophers have grappled with the problem of weighing arguments that are based on evaluations. Different systems have been developed for determining which of two arguments is more reasonable. One system will be described here. However, two cautions must be noted. First, remember that the decision to use this system represents an evaluation in itself. Other philosophers prefer different evaluation systems. Second, a subjective evaluation is also made when the total value of an argument is determined, and when two totals are compared.

The basic system for determining the total value of an argument and for comparing the total values of two arguments relies on three variables: the number of virtues directly satisfied, the number of evaluative categories addressed, and the relative importance of the standards involved.

We earlier described the reasons why Mr. Johnston placed his grandfather clock in his living room. First, the location satisfied his sense of propriety, a virtue included in personal truth. He was pleased that he was following the custom that his elders established. Second, the location of the clock satisfied the aesthetic virtues of balance, size, style, and color. Third, Mr. Johnston felt that the location was good in that the clock could be seen easily by family members and friends who might wish to know the time. The clock could inform more people in a public, rather than a private, room. The location allowed for the greatest benefit to the most people, thereby involving a virtue of social justice. We are convinced by Mr. Johnston's reasoning, because at least one virtue of personal truth, four virtues of aesthetic beauty, and one virtue of social justice are reflected. At least six virtues are directly satisfied. Three evaluative categories are addressed. In addition, social virtues are involved, which carry more weight than aesthetic virtues, which, in turn, carry more weight than personal virtues.

Moving from least important to most important, the system proceeds from evidential truth, to personal truth, to aesthetic beauty, to social justice, to religious justice. Personal taste can be supplemented by aesthetic beauty, social justice, and, ultimately, religious justice. People need to move beyond themselves when arguing, to consider the consequences of their choices on nature, the rights of other people, and on a transcendental power. People must be open-minded and attempt to construct or recognize alternative arguments, then to choose the most rational one. The most rational argument involves the greatest amount of goodness: the greatest value.

Language and Thought

Language and thought are the most wonderful and mysterious human characteristics. If we understood them better, we would be closer to an ideal definition of <u>human</u>. We would know more about our most sophisticated abilities. Since volumes of information have been published over the centuries about these fascinating subjects, it is impossible to comprehensively review conceptualizations of language and thought in a few textbook pages, so we will only address a few interesting questions. Know that our answers are shared by some authorities, but not all. We will tell you part of our theory of the world.

The first question we choose to explore is, "Can thought take place independently of language?" We believe it can. First, let's consider infants. Newborns do not come with a complete set of fully-functioning accessories, like an elaborate computer system. For example, newborns are not immediately familiar with the language system of the speech community into which they are born. Like an inexpensive computer system, infants have the potential to achieve greater capacity and performance. Infants think, perceive, make sense of the world, remember, and act purposefully without language. They do not seek language until after they have developed a generalization, hypothesis, or evaluation; and have learned that language exists, works systematically, and can be helpful. For infants, thought precedes language. Second, people can react physically or emotionally without language. We don't have to think, "I am listening to music," for us to know what is occurring. We could quickly turn down the volume if it was too high without using language to think, "That music is hurting my ears." We could turn down the volume if we did not enjoy the music without using language to think, "I don't like that music." Third, we can act without consciously being aware of language in our minds, as when we complete many motor functions. Football halfbacks do not have time to think words as they decide where to run so they don't get tackled, yet important spatial and physical decisions have to be made concerning angle, mass, velocity, proximity, and body position. As one famous halfback said while struggling to explain his success, "I guess I just run where they ain't!" Michelangelo did not think or write a detailed list of steps to follow and techniques to use as he sculpted David. In fact, when asked how he had accomplished his sculpture, Michelangelo simply stated that he saw David in the block of stone and chipped away everything that wasn't him. He knew it was finished when it looked finished. Inner speech is not necessary for all creative acts, although it can be helpful at times as we will describe later. Fourth, we all have experienced times when we wished to express an idea but couldn't put it into words. This problem would never arise, if thought were impossible without language. Fifth, we think it is preposterous to believe that the brain can control involuntary actions such as breathing without language, but not believe that the brain can control voluntary actions such as the formation of a generalization without language. Thought without conscious language use accounts for those instances when the resolution to a problem that we hadn't thought about for days suddenly pops into our consciousness and we shout, "Eureka!"

The second question we wish to ask is, "Even if language isn't necessary for thought to occur, can language be helpful?" We believe that language can be an important mediator. Language is a set of symbols that can be conveniently manipulated. Language represents something beyond itself. Language simplifies and clarifies thought. For example, when we use a term (a label) like chair, we immediately have an organizer that brings a multitude of previous experiences together. We have a generalization in mind that has been abstracted from the individual experiences we had with chairs. We do not have to sort through each experience with chairs. We use this category to help us identify and clarify by considering class inclusion. Thinking is slowed when we use language in conscious thought, because we have to attend to ideas and their expression in language. Thinking without language is purer and faster because we only have to attend to one thing at a time. Yet, it is frequently advantageous for us to slow our thinking. If we move cautiously and carefully control thought as we form hypotheses and evaluations, our arguments and conclusions will be clearer. Language slows our thinking and gives us greater control over our thoughts. We usually make better decisions when we take more time to collect evidence, form arguments, and decide on conclusions.

Language can be as helpful when we memorize as when we recall information from memory. When we wish to remember the names of the people whom we just met at a party, we often use language to help us. We repeat the people's names in our minds. We repeat new telephone numbers. We rehearse the lines we are supposed to speak in a play. Repetition breeds familiarity; familiarity breeds remembrance. Memory can also be enhanced when we use language to elaborate. For example, if we had to memorize the number 2618, we could change it to a different form that is easier to remember. We could call it, "twenty-six, eighteen; two thousand, six hundred and eighteen," or think of "two multiplied by three, multiplied by three again." When we take apart an unfamiliar machine, we try to remember the sequence for disassembly, so we can reverse the order and put parts where they belong when we reassemble. Language can help us elaborate and make the parts and order more memorable. We may say, "The object that looks like a snake goes on top, the part that looks like a doughnut goes in the middle, and the thing that looks like a brick goes on the bottom. Snake, doughnut, brick." It is easier to remember objects that look familiar, than objects that are unfamiliar. We will say more about mnemonic (memory) devices and elaboration in chapter #4 which concerns study strategies.

Language helps us regulate the behavior of others. We direct others when we command, "Sit down!" or "Please turn to page 53 in your workbook."

Finally, language helps us to communicate with others. When we use language to mediate our personal thinking we are communicating with ourselves. When we use language to convey our thoughts to other people, we are communicating with society. Verbal language is the most familiar, elaborate and sophisticated language that we can use to communicate with society, even though we can communicate through music, drama, art, and numbers. Humans have a basic need to communicate which is frequently satisfied best when verbal language is used. In fact, there is a question whether language would have developed at all if no two people ever met. We may never know the answer to that question, but we do know that society plays a large part in the formation and acquisition of language.

As mentioned earlier in this chapter, a society agrees to the assignment of referents to terms. It would be confusing if an object were called ten different names by ten different people. For example, that sandwich of heroic proportions made with hard-crusted bread, cheese, sauce, and varieties of cold meat is called a "poor boy" in New Orleans, a "grinder" in New England, a "hoagy" in Philadelphia, a "submarine" in California, and a "hero" in New York. Each speech community adopts phonemic, morphemic, semantic, and syntactic conventions to ease communication.

Language is a product of social interaction, and is learned through social interaction. Children must have sufficient contact with speakers in a particular speech community to acquire the language of that community. Children must be immersed in language activities, so they can discover the purpose and structure of language, and receive feedback as to the quality of their utterances.

Language is dynamic; it changes as it is used. It changes because it can be used creatively. The language of individuals and the language of a speech community change. In regard to individual use, language changes because of models we wish to emulate and because of our creative use of language. Socialization helps us acquire language, but we do not simply repeat sentences that we have heard. Our use of language is not merely repetitive. We are capable of producing novel utterances. We create many sentences as we speak normally that we have never heard. We move beyond the language we have heard by manipulating language and producing understandable sentences that are consistent with the language system in our speech community. We are not limited to parroting sentences we have heard. Individuals use language dynamically.

In regard to use within a speech community, language changes to accommodate new knowledge and taste. For example, as computer technology developed, American researchers felt they needed a term to describe the smallest unit of information in computers and communications theory. They contracted the terms "binary digit" into "bit." This is the same technique used to form the word laser. It was contracted from "light amplification by stimulated emission of radiation." The French realized that their language did not have terms that were equivalent in meaning to bit and laser. As a result, they borrowed the terms from English and refer to "le bit" and "le laser" to name the new concepts. At times, English has borrowed from French and other languages too. Sometimes new words are coined, as when the device we now call "television" was developed, and when "kleenex" was created. Television was derived from classic roots. Kleenex was an original word used by a single manufacturer because the sound was pleasing. In fact, the word was so appealing, that it became the standard word to use when referring to bathroom tissue. Sometimes additional meanings are given to existing terms. For example, chip did not refer to a tiny wafer on which electronic circuits are etched one hundred years ago. The new meaning was added because of an analogical similarity between a flattish fragment and a particular kind of computer circuit. Finally, language changes due to changes in taste. Language reflects the mood of a speech community. For example, it was acceptable for a time to use the word ain't, but now it ain't.

Conclusion

We covered a lot of territory in this important chapter. We quickly traveled through centuries of thought about epistemology, informal logic, and linguistics; and noted landmarks on the trail. We hope you completed the journey and benefitted. If you did, you will benefit more from the rest of the textbook, as the journey continues...

Introduction to Chapter #2

Reading is a complex and mysterious process which has been variously described. No definitive description of the reading process exists. As Edmund Huey explained, "...to completely analyze what we do when we read would indeed be the acme of a psychologist's achievements, for it would describe very many of the most intricate workings of the human mind as well as unravel the tangled story of the most remarkable specific performance that civilization has learned in all its history."[1] Despite the difficulty of the task, however, a prospective teacher must develop a personal understanding of the reading process, since a teacher's articulated or intuitive definition affects the objectives, methods, materials, and evaluation procedures that are used in the classroom.

---

[1]Edmund B. Huey, The Psychology and Pedagogy of Reading, (New York: Macmillan, 1908), p. 6.

Chapter 2

The Reading Process

Early in human history, attempts were made to communicate through graphic symbols since it was clear that aural/oral messages could not be preserved without great selectivity and effort. As an old Chinese proverb suggests, "The palest ink is better than the best memory." Graphic symbols offered an invariant, relatively permanent record that helped authors overcome spatial and temporal separation between themselves and their audiences. Graphic symbols also enabled readers to process a message at their own pace, unlike oral language where the rate at which a message was presented was determined by the discretion of the sender. Readers could regress to clarify, pause to reflect or rest, scan to locate specific information, and/or skim to concentrate on as much information as was needed to gain a general sense of the message.

Today, reading material is one of the most available, accessible, inexpensive, and satisfying media of communication. Reading is a meeting of the minds, an interaction between the thoughts of an author and the audience. An involved reader unleashes the powerful magic of the written word. The silent language of a printed page can scream for attention, prick the conscience, and comfort the soul.

Reading is thinking. Reading is reasoning. Reading is a decision-making process. Readers use their knowledge of generalizations, hypotheses, and evaluations to identify and resolve mysteries as they interact with printed symbols. However, before describing the process of reading in depth, we will explore the numerous variables which influence reading to expose you to the complexity and fragility of reading. Understanding is not always accomplished with ease, since print does not guarantee perfect communication. Print signals meaning; it does not contain meaning. Readers must construct meaning to the best of their abilities. Considering the complexities of people, reading processes, and printed materials; teachers should be surprised whenever a reader understands, not surprised when understanding is imperfect.

Variables That Influence Reading

Someone reads something somewhere. A lot of meaning is packed into that simple statement. First, an active reader must be involved, or no reading can take place. As a result, many variables that affect a person's physical, emotional, or mental condition can influence reading. Second, printed material must be present to provide a stimulus. As a result, textual characteristics influence a reader's understanding. Finally, reading occurs in an environment, such as a cold classroom or a warm bed. As a result, conditions outside of the reader and text may influence understanding.

Researchers have studied reading from numerous perspectives during the past century. As could be expected, researchers frequently examined the most obvious, manipulable variables, and less frequently examined subtler variables that required sophisticated instruments. Textual characteristics, such as the size and darkness of letters, were easier to manipulate than complex environments or the extremely complex human mind. In fact, very little, if any, research has actually examined the physiological changes that occur in the mind when a person is involved in reading. Physicians and physiologists are far from understanding the chemical, electrical, and mechanical changes that occur in the body and brain as people think and read. Teachers too are limited to observing overt manifestations of thinking and reading. People cannot observe thinking directly, so we make inferences based on the products of thinking: verbal responses, written answers, and physical actions.

Variables Associated With The Reader. Thinking can be fatiguing. Some people even find it more tiring to concentrate for a few hours than to exercise their large muscles for the same length of time. As a result, readers must have enough stamina to maintain intense attention and persevere. Stamina is developed through physical exercise, good nourishment, adequate rest, and timely medical care when we are temporarily ill; conditions that aren't necessarily satisfied by the typical teenager.

In addition to stamina, a person's physical potential must be considered. We all have limitations that can't always be overcome. Some of these limitations are inherited, while some result from inadequate development or physical injury. The organs that are most closely related to reading are the ears and the eyes. Auditory acuity, keenness of hearing, is important because we primarily learn language through our ears. Visual acuity, keenness of sight, is important because reading relies heavily on the processing of visual stimuli. However, we don't hear solely with our ears or see with our eyes. The brain hears and sees after receiving information from our sensory organs. The condition of the brain, therefore, is important. Even when our hearing and sight are normal, we may hear or see incorrectly due to distortion when discriminating. We may not hear the difference between "sip" and "zip" or see the difference when reading dad or dab. The brain perceives the incoming signal. Faulty perception may be due to inadequate knowledge, but it may also be due to organic dysfunction. For many years, reading authorities relied on some form of the term brain dysfunction to explain the cause of serious reading problems. No one really knows if that convenient explanation is valid, since teachers and physicians do not have highly accurate methods for diagnosing neurological and organic problems, or a complete understanding of the association between perceptual problems and reading problems. Yet, the explanation is plausible and can't be entirely ignored.

Teachers are not trained to be physicians, so they cannot treat organic problems. Teachers should, however, note symptoms of auditory and visual acuity problems so they can refer a child who they suspect of having difficulty to a medical authority. Symptoms of auditory disturbances can be grouped into three categories: 1) avoidance symptoms, such as in the case of the child who shuns listening tasks, 2) behavioral symptoms, such as inattention, tilting of the head, rubbing of the ears, or faulty pronunciation and intonation, and 3) complaints, such as earaches, buzzing, or dizziness. Symptoms of visual disturbances can be grouped into the same three categories: 1) avoidance symptoms, such as in the case of a child who shuns reading tasks or close visual work, 2) behavioral symptoms, such as squinting, fatigue, or excessive blinking, and 3) complaints, such as dizziness, redness of the eyes, blurring, or double vision.

Readers bring their emotions, as well as their physical characteristics, to the task of reading. In fact, no reading will occur unless people decide that it is worthwhile to read. We must accept the evaluation that reading can be beneficial. A reader must have a desirable purpose, or purposes, to achieve. An unmotivated person will not read at all, or will read ineffectively.

What emotions motivate people to read? When evaluations were discussed in the first chapter of this book, we said that normal people seek pleasure over pain. People try to satisfy their needs for happiness. In general, satisfactory purposes for reading can be broken into two categories, each of which contains two subcategories. Readers can read for pleasure; for personal enjoyment, or to entertain others. Readers can read for knowledge; for personal improvement, or to inform and guide others. We will give you examples of how reading satisfies needs that fall into these categories.

The need to escape can be satisfied by reading for personal enjoyment. When we want to escape, we crave to break loose from the confinement of boredom or oppressive circumstances. Escape, which brings relief and joy, can be made for relaxation or out of necessity. Journeys into fantasy worlds or the worlds of happier people are sometimes needed to break the malaise that accompanies insecurity, loneliness, and deprivation. Reading allows us to participate vicariously in events. Books can be a bloodless substitute for life. Reading allows for participation in events that are beyond the capabilities of the reader, occur in another person's life, are dangerous, or are removed in time or place. Vicarious experience satisfies the spirit and mind.

The need to bring happiness to others can be met by reading to entertain. We frequently please and amuse audiences when we read orally, or act in a play. In the case of reading for personal pleasure, individuals read to please themselves. When reading¹ to entertain, individuals are primarily concerned with pleasing others, although they may achieve personal satisfaction at the same time.

The need to learn can be satisfied by reading for personal improvement. We may learn to survive; to function at a minimal level of existence and effectiveness. Basic health, food, and safety needs can be met with greater ease when we can read the findings, recommendations, and cautions of others. In addition, we will be better citizens if we understand the important documents of our society which detail rights and responsibilities. We may learn to achieve; to move beyond mere survival and excel. We personally benefit as we learn more about the human condition through our explorations of psychology, biology, and philosophy. We also learn about aesthetic beauty, the advantages of social affiliation, and transcendental power as we read about the fine arts, government, and theology. We experience the personal satisfaction which comes as we strive to fulfill our potential by successfully completing a learning challenge. This is the joy of trying to be the best we can become.

The need to obtain valuable knowledge which can be brought to others can be satisfied by reading in preparation for teaching or testing. We often choose to learn the information that is needed to guide students. We ask, "Do I know what my students need to know?" because we can't teach what we don't know. Whereas reading for enjoyment or improvement is focused on an individual, reading to entertain or teach is focused on others. Good teacher education programs provide prospective teachers with most of the content that will need to be taught, but they cannot include everything, given time restrictions, and instructional expectations which vary by district and change over time. We also ask, "Do I know how to convey my knowledge?" As a result, educators study methods of teaching, since effective teaching serves others. As students or employees, we frequently complete reading assignments so we can inform teachers or employers of our knowledge when they test us. Although personal growth may result, our primary purpose is to prove to others that we learned, thereby informing and guiding teachers and employers as they assign grades, distribute honors, plan future lessons, decide on retention, award raises, and assign promotions.

Emotion can upset the reading process in two ways. First, readers may become so anxious that they are debilitated. Some anxiety is necessary to motivate us to work. That is why a few of us rely on procrastination to motivate us to read and study. We wait until the last minute to perform; when we can't ignore the possibility of failure which confronts us. Too much anxiety, however, may cause us to lose control. If our fear is overwhelming, we will not be able to read effectively. For example, we have all heard stories of intense high school geniuses who freeze and do poorly on the Scholastic Aptitude Test because they are so afraid that they won't score highly enough to get admitted to the college of their choice. Second, reading will be less effective when emotions force us to attend to other concerns than the reading task at hand. Reading suffers when we are distracted. We do not benefit fully from reading if our thoughts jump from the pages of a book to the beauty of the autumn leaves, or to our excitement over a romantic date. Emotions compete for attention.

Since emotions compete for attention, readers must be able to ignore emotions which lead them away from the intense concentration that is needed for reading and studying. Psychologists are far from knowing all the personal and social attitudes which hinder or aid reading. It is reasonable to believe, however, that low self-esteem will adversely affect a person's ability to learn or read effectively. People need to be convinced that they are capable and worthy of achieving success.

How does this self-esteem develop? As with all personal attitudes, they develop as an individual interacts with objects, events, and other people. It is difficult to separate personal and social experience. We become who we are in large part by interacting with others; we learn directly from others when they evaluate us, and when we rate ourselves in comparison to others. We may become angry with others and find that our hostility prevents us from attending to our own work. For example, many of us have experienced occasions when we got discouraged too quickly or burned so much nervous energy worrying about an injustice caused by a parent, teacher, or peer that we did not want to do the work that might please them. When the work went unaccomplished, we felt badly about ourselves since we left important work undone, and because we were not able to overcome the frustration that prevented us from coping with the situation in a more productive way. In the end we suffered, because we were disappointed in ourselves.

In addition to physical and emotional condition, a person's mental condition must be considered. Two important components of mental condition will be stressed: background knowledge and memory. Understanding is primarily influenced by knowledge that people have gained through prior experience. The more readers know, the easier it will be for them to understand. What do readers need to know? Readers need to know generalizations, hypotheses, and evaluations: descriptions, explanations, and judgements. Some of this knowledge relates to content areas, and some relates to language. Readers will not find textbooks that are densely packed with key concepts difficult to understand or remember, if they already know many of the concepts or related concepts. It is also crucial that people be adept at using language if they are to be good readers, since reading is a language process.

People naturally develop an awareness of language through listening and speaking. This serves as a foundation on which the more advanced language abilities of reading and writing are built. As people read they use their knowledge of phonology, orthography, typography, morphology, semantics, syntax, and rhetoric. Phonology is the study of language sounds. Linguists believe that approximately 44 sounds are used in English. For example, knowing that the sound you hear at the beginning of band is the same sound that you hear at the beginning of bank displays phonological knowledge.

Orthography is the study of spelling patterns. Orthographic knowledge includes familiarity with homonyms and homographs; words that sound alike but are spelled differently (pear-pair-pare), and words that are spelled alike but that have different pronunciations (read: /red/ and /ri:d/, minute: /'minit/ and /mai'nju:t/). In its most advanced form, orthography examines intraword redundancies; restraints on spelling within words. For example, when a fluent reader sees a three letter word that begins with a t and an h, the reader knows that the last letter must either be e or y (the, thy). The fluent reader intuitively knows that the last letter must be a vowel, and that only e and y are acceptable in this case.

Typography is the study of the physical characteristics of print. Knowing that i in manuscript is the same letter as i in cursive, and that 2 in Arabic style is the same as II in Roman style are examples of typographical knowledge. Typography shows us the shapes of printed letters and numbers. Typography also shows us spacing, margins, direction (left-to-right, top-to-bottom in English), capitalization marks and punctuation marks.

Morphology is the study of the smallest units of meaning in language. Types of morphemes include inflectional endings, tense markers, and the roots to which they are attached. Knowing that s signifies plurality when it is attached to <u>pan</u>, as in <u>pans</u>, is an example of morphemic knowledge.

Semantics is the study of the meanings of terms. Semanticists study the areas that are listed below and others:

--univocal and equivocal terms. Univocal terms have a single meaning like <u>photosynthesis</u>, and equivocal terms have multiple meanings such as <u>set</u>.

--denotative and connotative meanings. For example, <u>ghost</u> specifically refers to the appearance of the spirit of a dead person, but it also implies fear. An emotional feeling is attached to the primary meaning of the term. Denotative meaning concerns the referent, while connotative meaning concerns the emotion which is evoked by the referent.

--concrete and abstract referents. A concrete term, such as <u>desk</u>, refers to a material object. An abstract term, such as <u>love</u>, refers to an idea that exists in minds.

--synonymity and antonymity. Synonymity is the similarity in meaning between two words; such as <u>big</u> and <u>huge</u>. Antonymity is the opposition in meaning between two words; such as <u>night</u> and <u>day</u>.

Syntax concerns the arrangement of words in a sentence. Syntactic generalizations describe acceptable prose sentences in a language or dialect. For example, adjectives must be placed before, not after, the nouns they modify in English. We can talk about a "red ball," but not about a "ball red." A sentence in English must have at least a subject and a verb. Sentences can be stated actively or passively; as in "The man walked the dog" and "The dog was walked by the man."

Rhetorical patterns are the conventional structures that authors use to write paragraphs and longer passages. For example, a paragraph or passage may start by stating a conclusion (generalization, hypothesis, or evaluation) and finish by listing the evidence which supports the conclusion. This structure is often found in reverse; the evidence is presented before the conclusion is stated. Most often, authors simply state their conclusions: generalizations, hypotheses, or evaluations. Later in this chapter when we talk about the characteristics of printed text, we will detail the rhetorical patterns that are emphasized in the various subject areas.

Memory is the second aspect of mental condition. Learning cannot be accomplished without remembering past knowledge, and without the ability to store the new knowledge that is obtained. How much information can be stored in memory? The answer to this question depends on how long people wish to remember information. Numerous experimental observations have shown that people can keep about seven pieces of information in immediate memory. The information can be numbers, letters, terms, or conclusions. For example, we would be able to remember the sequence 5-9-1-3-7-1-5 easier than 5-9-1-3-7-1-4-2-8-5. It is not merely coincidental that telephone numbers are seven numbers long, and that zip codes of five numbers are remembered easier than zip codes of nine numbers. Information in immediate memory is quickly lost, unless we take steps to retain the information for a significantly longer time. If we sufficiently rehearse and possibly elaborate the information in immediate memory, it enters long term memory from where it can be retrieved hours, days, or possibly years after it was learned. We know the information so well, that it stays with us longer. The storage capacity of long term memory is not known, although it must be enormous, since every person knows an incredibly large amount of information. It is difficult to investigate the capacity of long term memory, since it varies considerably among individuals, and since researchers have no way of knowing if unretrievable information has been simply forgotten, has become impossible to retrieve, or has been necessarily forced from memory and replaced by new information.

There are two keys to good memory. First, a person has to be selective. People cannot remember everything that they sense. A learner must acquire the ability to attend to the most relevant information and ignore the less relevant information. Instead of remembering Shelley, Keats, Johnson, Faulkner, Twain, and Hemingway; it may be enough to remember that the information presented was about British and American authors. Second, learners must try to remember the largest chunks of information that they can manage. Instead of trying to remember 1-3-5-7-9-1-3, 2-4-6-8-2-4-6, 11-13-15-17-19-11-13, and 12-14-16-18-12-14-16, the information can be remembered in simpler form by grouping it into larger categories. In this case, we could think about "seven odd numbers under 10, even numbers under 10, odd numbers between 10 and 20, and even numbers between 10 and 20." More is remembered from less.

As you have just seen, reading starts with people who bring their physical, emotional, and mental characteristics to the task. In the next section of this chapter, we will discuss the characteristics of the materials that people might read.

Variables Associated With The Text. A printed source must be available for a person to read. People can read signs, newspapers, magazines, novels, plays, poetry, reference books, textbooks, and handwritten notes: anything with conventional numbers, letters, and other symbols. Characteristics of the material to be read influence a person's ability to reconstruct and understand the author's message.

We will primarily describe the textual characteristics of books that are traditionally used in classrooms, and will briefly mention the characteristics of other types of reading material. We simply mention other types of reading material to encourage you to use a variety of materials in your classrooms. Variety breaks monotony. Variety can be used to reinforce, reteach, or enrich. In addition, materials such as newspapers, magazines, and journals provide the most current information available, while reference books are rich repositories of valuable information from the past.

Printed materials must be presented in language which is familiar to the intended audience, or confusion may result. Obviously, a book would not be printed in Russian, if it were intended for an American audience. Less extreme cases, however, may present problems. In the first case, material written in an unfamiliar dialect may not be immediately understandable to speakers of "Standard English," the dialect that is most popular among the cultural majority in America. (ex., He be goin' Monday week. = He will be going next Monday.) This generalization also applies in reverse: dialect speakers might have difficulty understanding material that is written in Standard English.

In the second case, materials written in language used hundreds of years ago may be difficult for a modern reader to understand. The Old English lines, "Come on wanre night scrida sceadugenga./ Came through the wan night slithering the shadow-thing." written around 1,000 A.D. may not be immediately understood in today's parlance as "Like was he (Satan) to the light stars;/ The laud (praise) of the ruler ought he to have wrought."[2] Spelling, usage, and meaning commonly change as years pass.

In a third case, readers may have difficulty understanding materials written in an unfamiliar mode of discourse. For example, if readers are used to expository materials, they may not immediately adjust to poetry, since poets alter sound, rhythm, and metaphors to convey their messages. Poetic license allows poets to

---

[2]Helen Laird and Charlton Laird, The Tree of Language, (Cleveland: World Publishing Company, 1957), p. 36.

be unconventional. Unconventionality can be innovative, effective, and beautiful.

In a fourth case, material that includes numerous abstract terms may be difficult to understand. Abstract terms refer to ideas that are products of the mind. Philosophical materials contain many abstract terms. In part, difficulty in understanding may be due to a lack of experience. Students have less experience with the ideas of other people than with objects and actions in the concrete, external world. That is why educators believe that abstract ideas are easier to understand when an author relates them to concrete ideas. In addition, understanding may be beyond the abilities of some students. Thinking about abstract ideas is a sophisticated activity that average people are only capable of completing about the time they become teenagers, according to such famous psychologists as Piaget and Bruner.

In a fifth case, language may be unfamiliar to an audience, even when it describes concrete experience. The experience may be completely new and unknown to the reader, or it may require a deeper understanding than the reader has developed through previous experience. For example, students may not adequately understand cell, tissue, and organ until living matter is studied in a biology class. Materials read by secondary students often present ideas in new and different ways; otherwise, there wouldn't be anything to learn. Books would just rehash information that students already know.

In a sixth case, the language may use notational symbols that are different from letters and words. Mathematics rely heavily on numbers, operational signs, equivalency signs, computer commands, and equations. The natural sciences use numbers, equations, and abbreviations for elements, states, and forces. Musical compositions are written with notes, scales, and bars. Choreographic scripts use special symbols to designate dance steps.

Typical textbooks use formats that provide convenient and helpful information that complements the body of the text. Effective textbooks are "user-friendly," to borrow a term from computing. The title, copyright date, author, and publisher are always listed. Additional information may be provided in a preface, annotations, reference lists, maps, graphs, tables, illustrations, and diagrams. Study aids may be offered in the form of a table of contents, glossary, index, introductions to chapters, headings, chapter summaries, exercises for review or enrichment, and terms that are emphasized in boldface or italic print. Readers must know how to benefit from these textual characteristics.

While textbooks are usually sequenced as chapters that build on one another, newspapers and magazines are not. Newspapers take many different forms, as do magazines. It is difficult to generalize as to their organization. Newspapers may order sections on such topics as politics, crime, business, entertainment, sports, fashion, cooking, social events, and real estate in various ways. The sequence of articles in a magazine is also casually related.

Five points about the features of newspapers, however, should be emphasized. First, articles do not always begin and end on the same page. Necessary cues are provided to direct a reader to an article's continuation. Second, the size of the headline and the location frequently point to the relative importance of an article. Third, advertisements are mixed with articles written by employees of the newspaper. Advertisements are normally separated from articles by clear borders, so that readers do not confuse the two. Fourth, cartoons, crossword puzzles, television schedules, and classified advertisements demand that different reading approaches be used than those used to read a standard article. For example, classified advertisements require that readers understand cryptic abbreviations. Fifth, newspapers are not written strictly to conform to an estimate of the intellectual level of the audience; as are textbooks for secondary students. The level of conceptual difficulty varies more greatly within a newspaper than in a textbook.

Like newspapers, magazine articles may be continued on later pages, advertisements are distinctly separated from articles, and articles are not strictly written to conform to an estimate of the intellectual ability of the audience. Unlike newspapers, magazines emphasize their statements of ownership, take pains to increase the helpfulness of their tables of content, and often provide referenced lists of advertisers.

Rhetorical patterns are also textual characteristics. Rhetorical patterns are the conventional structures which authors use to convey their messages. In English, a short story or novel often introduces the important characters, notes a conflict, describes attempts to resolve the conflict, details the resolution of the conflict, and finally connects loose ends. The story expressed in a play is developed in much the same way as in a short story or novel, but dialogue carries the story in a play. Little or no narrative is included. In addition, a play includes stage directions: descriptions of scenes and movements. Poems often use conventional rhythms, rhyme schemes, line and stanza lengths, and divisions. For example, a Shakespearean sonnet is a fourteen line poem, with three stanzas of four lines and a concluding couplet, with a formal pattern of rhymes, written in iambic pentameter.

In the social sciences, information is often presented in chronological order, or as an argument that supports a hypothesis regarding a causal relationship.

In mathematics, authors primarily rely on generalizations, since mathematics includes systems of definition. Arithmetic, geometry, and calculus, for example, proceed from primary generalizations to functional generalizations, from definitions of terms to definitions of relationships among the terms. Math textbooks also are distinctive in their heavy reliance on numerical and word problems that need to be completed by students.

In natural science textbooks, authors often define primary, functional, and statistical generalizations. Authors frequently describe experiments, which are arguments that support generalizations and hypotheses: descriptions and explanations.

In the fine arts, musical compositions make numerous demands on readers. Specific types of orchestral composition have unique formal structures that help readers follow and evaluate. A fugue, for example, is a musical composition in which one or more themes are introduced and then repeated in a complex pattern. A song presents musical notes and words on different lines that readers must process in a coordinated manner. Art history books often present arguments supporting elaborate evaluations of aesthetic beauty in chronological sequence. Books concerning artistic techniques describe detailed procedures in sequence. If you wish to consider a product of art (ex., drawing, painting, sculpture, or pot) to be an object that can be read, then we could speak about visual literacy. People are visually literate if they understand the structures of artistic creations. When examining a painting, we could investigate color, shape, line, light, texture, pattern, perspective, point of view, size, framing, motion, sequence, and juxtaposition.

In the mechanical and procedural arts, such as automotive mechanics, home economics, driver education and gymnastics, authors tend to present generalizations in hierarchical order. That is, after introducing equipment, simple procedures are described before more complex procedures are presented. An automotive mechanic will be taught about common bolts, sockets, and ratchets before being given the sequence of actions to follow to replace and tighten a steel bolt. Additionally, this instruction will precede instruction in replacing a delicate alloy bolt with special sockets and a torque wrench.

Variables Associated With The Environment. Remember that someone reads something somewhere. People read at home, school, and on playgrounds. Ideally, people will find the trust, respect, nourishment, guidance, knowledge, and encouragement from parents, teachers, siblings, and peers that are needed to promote effective reading. An atmosphere filled with fear and frustration is not emotionally healthy. In this section we will discuss the two most important environments in which people may read: home and school.

When reading and studying at home, students do best when their parents and siblings are supportive, and when their rooms have comfortable temperatures. Ideally too, students should find models and resources in the home environment that encourage reading. Students will be more interested in reading if they see their siblings and parents benefitting from reading. Students will read more if newspapers, magazines, and books are readily available at home.

Students face much more complicated environments when reading and studying at school, than when working at home. Educators rarely appreciate the complexity of learning at school. Teachers are extremely presumptuous. We presume that students want to learn what we want them to learn, when we want them to learn, in the manner we want them to learn, for as long as we want them to learn, and from us. Students may not be interested in a topic. Students may not wish to explore a topic to the depth that we want to take them. Students may not be interested or energetic at the particular time information is presented, or may not be intellectually or physically advanced enough to benefit from the instruction when it is given. Students may not like the materials or methods we use to teach. Students may not wish to invest as much time as we demand. The most shocking case, however, is when students refuse to learn because they reject our personality or have a low opinion of our professional competencies.

No one knows how many students refuse to learn, or learn less well, because they dislike their teachers. Student-teacher conflicts occur everyday, but it is difficult to judge how dramatically these conflicts affect learning. It is easy to understand the difficulty of having successful student-teacher matches when you consider the number and varieties of personalities involved. A typical secondary student may interact with six or seven teachers each day. A typical secondary teacher may interact with 150-200 students each day.

Let's examine the personalities of teachers. A persistent myth discounts the influences that the problems and personality of a teacher have on the learning process. As Greene explains,

Lecturers seem to presuppose a 'man within a man' when they

describe a good teacher as infinitely controlled and accommodating, technically efficient, impervious to moods. They are likely to define him by the role he is <u>expected</u> to play in a classroom, with all his loose ends gathered up and all his doubts resolved. The numerous realities in which he exists as a living person are overlooked. His personal biography is overlooked; so are the many ways in which he expresses his private self in language, the horizons he perceives, the perspectives through which he looks on the world.[3]

Teachers <u>do</u> bring their financial, medical, marital, social, and emotional problems to school. Teachers do not cease to be human when they walk through the doors to their classrooms. Teachers are not automatons and cannot routinely be expected to act perfectly or dispassionately. To illustrate how a problem can affect the performance of a teacher, let's explore the psychological concept of alienation.

Alienation consists of five components: powerlessness, meaninglessness, normlessness, isolation, and self-estrangement.[4] Teachers who feel powerless believe that they cannot affect change. Teachers who experience meaninglessness feel that their lives and work are worthless. Feelings of normlessness reflect a basic lack of values and goals in teachers' lives. Isolation occurs when teachers feel that their lives and work go unrecognized and unsupported. Self-estrangement occurs when teachers feel forced to play roles that hide their true selves. Clearly, any form of alienation will dampen a teacher's outlook on life and will lessen efforts in the classroom. Teachers must do their best to recognize, understand, and control the problems that life throws in their paths, so that those problems do not adversely affect students. Teachers must understand themselves before they can understand and serve others.

What are the personal characteristics of effective teachers? What traits should people who wish to teach hope to find in themselves? A plethora of research studies have been conducted in an effort to identify the characteristics of ideal teachers. Unfortunately, the results are inconclusive. On the one hand, we find authorities who believe that effective teachers possess good intrapersonal

---

[3]Maxine Green, <u>Teacher or Stranger</u>, (Belmont, Ca.: Wadsworth, 1973), pp. 269-270.

[4]M. Seeman, "On the Meaning of Alienation," <u>American Sociological Review</u> 24 (December 1959):783-791.

and interpersonal skills; skills that facilitate living effectively with oneself and others. In other words, good people make good teachers. On the other hand, we find comments like the following which were taken from a study that compared teachers who had been classified as successful and unsuccessful:

> It is a common belief that only normal, well-adjusted persons should be teachers. But some of the successful teachers observed were definitely neurotic, and their neuroticism contributed to their success as teachers. Here is a teacher who is obviously compulsive-obsessional. She puts great emphasis on order, accuracy, precision, and she is teaching children to order their lives. Here is another teacher with an overdeveloped conscience who teaches her pupils to distinguish right from wrong. Here is another teacher with a need to dominate who vigorously carries children along with her own high standards of achievement. Here is a teacher with masochistic tendencies who whips herself by the long hours and hard work she puts into the job. These neurotic teachers may not fit every type of situation but if they can find the right place they can be highly constructive influences.[5]

What can we conclude about the personal characteristics of effective teachers? It is probably safe to say that well-adjusted people who have the ability to relate to others have a greater chance of succeeding as teachers. However, when considering the needs of certain students, teachers with atypical characteristics may be more successful.

What professional competencies must successful teachers have to use reading to teach? Broadly speaking, teachers must understand the typical characteristics of the age groups they instruct. Teachers must understand the common physical, intellectual, emotional, and social characteristics of the students they serve. This information, usually covered in educational or developmental psychology courses, acts as a baseline to which the characteristics of individuals can be compared. In this way, teachers can understand individual differences; ways in which people deviate from the average. Teachers must also be familiar with the content they wish to teach, and with instructional strategies for promoting effective reading. Subject matter knowledge is developed through independent, undergraduate, and graduate studies. Knowledge of instructional strategies which teachers can use to help typical students read content area

---

[5]Percival Symonds, "Reflections on Observations of Teachers," Journal of Educational Research 43 (May 1950):688-696.

materials more effectively will be described later in chapter #5. Before describing methods for stimulating effective reading, however, we must describe the reading process in greater depth than we have before in this book.

A Description Of The Reading Process

Many reading authorities have offered elaborate theoretical models of reading. An interesting collection of these models is contained in Theoretical Models and Processes in Reading.[6] There could never be a single, simple description of reading, since there are many different types of reading, and different types of readers. For example, the process a reader uses to find a number in a telephone book is different from the process of previewing a textbook to get a general sense of its content. In addition, there are differences between the processes primary grade students use when they begin to learn to read, and the processes that are used by secondary students who have severe problems with reading. In this section, we will only describe the process that a fluent, effective reader uses. We will describe what happens when everything goes well, since this is the condition teachers hope to promote in their students.

Reading is thinking. Reading is reasoning. Reading is a decision-making process. Readers use their knowledge of generalizations, hypotheses, and evaluations to identify and resolve mysteries as they interact with printed symbols.

Readers must first decide whether it is worthwhile to make a commitment to read. A reader must ask, "How will I benefit from reading?" A reader must have a desirable purpose, or purposes, to achieve. An unmotivated reader will not read at all, or will read ineffectively. Readers may choose to read for enjoyment, entertainment, personal improvement, or to guide others. A reader needs to identify a worthwhile purpose for completing a reading task, then decide to enthusiastically undertake the task. For example, a history buff may decide to learn more about World War I.

Once the decision to read has been made, readers clarify their goal(s). A reader asks, "What specific information do I want to learn?" For example, the reader may wish to learn the author's explanation of the causes of the war and the names of the famous generals who fought; an argument which proves a

---

[6]Harry Singer and Robert Ruddell, eds., Theoretical Models and Processes of Reading, 3rd edition, (Newark, Del.: International Reading Association, 1985).

hypothesis, and generalizations.

Now that the reader knows what needs to be learned, the reader can ask, "What do I already know?" This brings the reader's prior knowledge to bear. The reader, in this case, may determine that only one cause of the war is known (the rising tide of nationalism), and that no generals are known.

Next, readers ask, "What might the text be able to offer?" Readers begin to interact with the text at this point. Readers look for important information such as the title, copyright date, and author; important sections such as a preface, table of contents, glossary, index, and annotations; graphic aids such as maps, diagrams, graphs, tables, and illustrations; and study aids such as chapter summaries, lists of references, and exercises.

Once motivated readers have determined what they want to learn, what is already known, and what the text in hand might offer, they can develop initial strategies for reading and remembering. These strategies comprise a structured approach to study which lead to improved understanding and retention. A structured approach is so important, that it must be determined before, rather than after, a careful reading occurs. Readers ask; "How fast should I read the material? At what level should I begin to sample the text?" and "What technique(s) will I use to emphasize important information?" The reader might decide to begin sampling a chapter by previewing the headings, introduction, and summary, and might decide to aid review and retention by underlining key words and phrases.

If uncertainty about the message is still present after the initial sampling, readers decide to spend more time with the text by sampling from it further. Readers intensely concentrate on the text. Readers use their knowledge to reconstruct and understand the author's message, and to regulate thinking. In other words, readers think, and think about thinking; processes that psychologists call cognition and metacognition respectively. As readers ask, "Do I understand the message?" they are reflecting on the author's generalizations, hypotheses, evaluations, and arguments. As readers ask, "What information do I still need to know and how will I get it?" they are regulating their thinking. Effective readers are sensitive to these monitoring and regulating functions and automatically make thousands of decisions as they read, without consciously asking themselves questions.

One of the decisions readers make as they decide where to find needed information concerns the level at which they must sample the text. Readers continuously review the decision to sample a text at a given level and decide if a greater level of sampling would be helpful. They may move beyond an examination of the headings, introduction, and summary to an examination of selected paragraphs, sentences, or words. They may go further by reading every word and every paragraph in sequence, stopping to examine word parts such as affixes, roots, letter clusters, and individual letters if they don't instantly recognize a word on sight. Readers only rely on print to the extent that it is necessary. If they can easily understand an author's message to the degree that suits their purpose, they don't have to read many words. They can reconstruct the message using a small sample of words. If they do not know anything about an author's message or have extreme difficulty in understanding the message, they may not even be helped by enumeration, by examining every spot of ink on the page.

Let's examine this brief description of the reading process in greater depth, since we do not want to leave you with the impression that reading proceeds in a linear manner. A reader is not like a sausage machine that receives raw material and processes it in a uniform series of steps until the final product results. An effective reader must be active and flexible in responding to the text and environment. Readers change their processing strategies depending on their purposes and the demands of the text and environment, just as people change their thinking as they attempt to make sense of the world in other instances. Reading is thinking, a meaning-seeking activity, an adaptive pursuit, a decision-making process that helps us make sense of the world. The world, in reading, is the text. Readers must reduce uncertainties, solve mysteries, that are presented by a text. This is accomplished, like any other thinking activity, by applying and developing generalizations, hypotheses, and evaluations. Application and development operate by comparing and contrasting, by collecting enough evidence until we are willing to risk being wrong, and by putting information into the broadest categories that are appropriate and manageable so that we do not overload memory.

Hypotheses and evaluations are extremely important in reading, but are used less frequently than generalizations. Readers spend most of their efforts deciding what something is, rather than why it is, or what good it is. Readers spend more time identifying a word for example, then explaining why that particular word was selected by a speech community to symbolize a concept, or then judging whether the author would have expressed the message more effectively with a different word choice.

Generalizations are developed and applied at all levels of language:

phonological, orthographical, typographical, morphological, syntactic, semantic, and rhetorical. For example, at the typographical level, we may use a generalization to decide if what we are looking at is another example of the letter b. Generalizations reduce uncertainty by eliminating alternatives. We know that b is similar to d because they are the same height and width, and because they both have a straight line and a closed curve. Our generalization, however, tells us that the first letter is a b because b is distinguished from d by having the closed curve on the right side of the line, instead of on the left. The generalization gives us adequate information to recognize the letter b in this context, where the only two choices considered are b and d. Other alternatives could have made recognition less difficult, or more difficult. Recognition would have been less difficult if we thought the letter was either b or w, since this maximal contrast is easy to distinguish. Recognition would have been more difficult if we thought the letter was either b, d, or p, since this minimal contrast would require that we use additional information; knowing that the straight line in b rises above the closed curve, while the straight line in p falls below the closed curve, even though the closed curve is on the right side of the line in both cases. Recognition would have been more difficult if we had to choose from numerous alternatives in a context, such as choosing b from among d, p, q, g, h, a, and c. Remember that the adequacy of our generalizations depends on the complexity of the context in which a problem is presented.

At the word level, a description of visual appearance is part of the generalization for a word. Through experience, readers compare and contrast words and identify their distinctive visual features. Goal does not look the same as coal, when considering the shape of the first letter and its contribution to the overall shape of the word. Effective readers use visual information economically. They learn to distinguish words based on minimal clues, the most crucial differences between words. After studying a word, readers learn what critical feature or features to focus on to identify the word. The word no longer has to be seen letter by letter. In part, this helps explain why some effective readers may not be effective spellers. Remember that it is easier to recognize than to recall. Less information is needed to identify something that exists, than is needed to bring something to existence. That may be why people write a word on a piece of scrap paper to see if it "looks right" if they are unsure how to spell the word. It is easier to recognize than to create.

At broader levels, readers learn the visual appearance, the typographical characteristics, of sentences, paragraphs, and chapters. The first word in a sentence begins with a capital letter, and the sentence ends with a punctuation mark. Of course, an exception to this generalization is when a sentence of dialogue begins with a quotation mark and ends with two punctuation marks, the last one being another quotation mark. Sentences are also separated from each other by greater spacing than is found between letters or words. Paragraphs are distinguished from each other either by indentation of the first line, or greater spacing than is found between lines. Chapters are primarily distinguished by their titles: names or numbers in a conventional location. Often, but not always, a chapter begins on a new page with its title at the top.

At the semantic level, generalizations are used to recognize differences in meaning. Walk and stroll both refer to a locomotive action; yet walk implies an ordinary pace, while stroll implies a leisurely pace.

At the rhetorical level, generalizations help readers distinguish between patterns; such as one which begins with a conclusion and follows with supportive evidence, as opposed to one which begins with the supportive evidence and finally states a conclusion.

Readers coordinate the use of generalizations in all levels of language as they read, since each area can provide clues that help solve mysteries, reduce uncertainties. Readers combine generalizations from these various areas as necessary. For example, a reader may use phonological, orthographical, typographical, syntactic, and semantic generalizations to read the last word in the sentence, "The football player kicked a field g___." Given knowledge of syntax, the reader would know that the last word in the sentence has to be a noun. The rules of word order reduce uncertainty by constraining the part of speech that is acceptable at a particular point in a sentence. Given knowledge of semantics, the reader would know that a particular game is being played, a participant is on the offense, the participant kicked the ball, and that the successful kick is probably labeled with a specialized term that refers to a score worth three points since the term punt does not appear, and field is the first part of the technical term field goal. The reader might decide that there is enough evidence to risk completing the sentence by reading "goal," or may seek additional evidence. If additional evidence is sought, phonological, orthographical, and typographical knowledge would tell the reader that the last word should start with the sound /g/ if the term is field goal, the letter associated with this sound is g, and that the word should have few letters. At this point, the reader might see the letter g and the shortness of the word, and decide that there is enough evidence to risk reading "goal."

The example that was just described concerns the recognition of a word (goal) in the context of a sentence. The sentence was packed with helpful syntactic and semantic clues that make it easier to recognize the word goal than if the word appeared in isolation. Readers do not always benefit, however, from available contextual clues, whether they are in the same sentence as the unknown word or in sentences that came before. When this happens, readers must take a new tact. Readers may skip the word and continue reading, hoping that information in future sentences will bear on the recognition of the unknown word, or hoping that the loss of meaning will be insignificant. Readers may ask a parent, teacher, or peer to tell them the word. Readers may find the word in a dictionary, if they know how to use a dictionary. Often, however, readers immediately approach an unknown word in context as if it were in isolation. Syntactic and semantic clues are not available at all to the reader when a word appears by itself. If a reader does not instantly recognize the visual features of goal when it is seen in isolation, then examination must be made below the word level.

As a result, typographical, phonological, and orthographical clues must be used. After noting the g, the reader may associate it with the sounds /g/ and /j/. After noting the vowel digraph oa, the reader may apply the generalization, "When two vowels appear in sequence, the long sound associated with the first vowel should be pronounced." You may have learned this generalization in elementary school as, "When two vowels go awalking, the first vowel does the talking, and the second one is silent." The reader decides that the second sound in the word may be /o/. After deciding that /o/ follows g, the reader would apply the generalization that g is associated with /g/ instead of /j/ when followed by /o/. After identifying the last letter, the reader may associate it with the sound /l/. Finally, the reader blends the sounds together /gol/ and uses previous knowledge to decide that the word must be goal, a word that has been heard and remembered from before. Now that the label for a concept has been decoded, the reader can bring forth whatever knowledge of the concept that is in mind. However, pronunciation does not guarantee understanding. A person may pronounce the nonsense word itchnotbog or the real word ratiocination without concepts in mind that are assigned to these labels.

Unfortunately, the strategic use of letter-sound associations is not exceptionally helpful, particularly for secondary school students. The use of letter-sound associations is commonly called phonics and is combined with information about morphemes in the category called structural analysis. One of the classic debates in the field of reading deals with the effectiveness and advisability of teaching readers to analyze the parts of words using typographical, orthographical, phonological, and morphological clues. Research studies support the low utility of structural generalizations. Spache summaries by stating that less than ten of the 121 different generalizations found in the literature lead to correct pronunciation of word parts at least 75 percent of the time.[7] In other words, the numerous generalizations are extremely unreliable. As the poem below illustrates, the irregularities in English can be frustrating. At times, it seems that there are more nonexamples than examples of a generalization. The studies Spache summarizes looked at words taught in popular instructional reading programs developed for elementary school students, yet the studies pertain to secondary school students, since the common words initially taught continue to appear in reading materials intended for secondary school students. Numerous studies have shown that morphemic generalizations succeed at a slightly higher rate in leading to correct pronunciation, and have the additional benefit of offering clues to meaning, but the level of consistency is not overwhelmingly impressive. Typographical, orthographical, phonological, and morphological generalizations can be used to reduce uncertainty, but only to a small degree.

Our Queer Lingo

When the English tongue we speak
Why is "break" not rhymed with "freak?"
Will you tell me why it's true
We say "sew," but likewise "few?"
And the maker of a verse
Cannot rhyme his "horse" with "worse?"

"Beard" is not the same as "heard;"
"Cord" is different from "word;"
"Cow" is cow but "low" is low;
"Show" is never spelled like "foe."
Think of "hose" and "dose" and "lose;"
And think of "goose" and yet of "choose;"
Think of "comb" and "tomb" and "bomb"
"Doll" and "roll" and "home" and "some."
And since "pay" is rhymed with "say"
Why not "paid" with "said," I pray?

Think of "blood" and "food" and "good;"
"Mould" is not pronounced like "could."

---

[7]George Spache, Diagnosing and Correcting Reading Disabilities, (Boston: Allyn and Bacon, 1976), p. 219.

Wherefore "done," but "gone" and "lone"
Is there any reason known?

To sum up all, it seems to me
Sounds and letters don't agree.

--anonymous

Additional problems are presented when words are analyzed; examined in pieces. Even if readers knew all of the moderately helpful orthographical, phonological, and morphological generalizations, and were adept at knowing when to use them; their consciousness and immediate memory would become so overloaded by attending to the application of generalizations that they would not be able to attend to or remember the meanings of words. Reading would be painfully slow and unproductive. Effective readers avoid these problems by recognizing words as quickly as possible. Effective readers do not read a word by examining it letter by letter. They take the entire word into consideration and only sample enough of the word to decide that they are looking at the word they think they see. Effective readers quickly switch their attention from word recognition to meaning, so they concentrate on the message and not the messenger.

We have established that generalizations regarding structural analysis are not especially helpful to secondary school students, since a reliance on these generalizations leads students away from meaning and forces them to use a slow, ineffective approach. The small benefit that might be obtained is not worth the great cost. In addition, we argue against a reliance on structural analysis when we describe the difficulty that some students have in making and using generalizations regarding the structure of words. High school sophomores, for example, have spent nine or ten years reading words from which they could have drawn structural generalizations. The students may have also received direct instruction to help them learn such generalizations. The students who did not benefit from ten years of opportunity or instruction probably will not suddenly start to understand these concepts with a few more months of reading or teaching. Secondary students must be encouraged to recognize whole words instantly, so they can quickly move to meaning.

Three important points need to be made. First, effective readers must know thousands of generalizations about language. It is not necessary, however, for readers to articulate their knowledge. It is only important that they can successfully use their knowledge. For example, children begin kindergarten knowing most of the phonological and syntactic rules of speech. They speak using the sounds of their speech community and use acceptable sentence structures, yet they could not state rules such as, "I use the sound /sh/ at the beginning of the term shampoo., A noun refers to a person, place, event, or object., An adjective must be placed before the noun it modifies.," or "A sentence must have a subject and a verb."

Second, readers are rarely consciously aware of the decision-making processes that they use as they try to understand. The example in the preceding paragraph of the thinking a reader might use while processing the sentence about the football player is highly artificial. Most of the coordination of knowledge is accomplished at a level below conscious awareness. Remember that in the first chapter we established that minds can work without having to use language as a mediator. In fact, people would be slowed to intolerable levels of processing if we had to be consciously aware of every decision that we made while reading. It is difficult, however, to know when our subconscious is thinking about a particular problem or when it is attending to another concern. When an idea seems to come to us from nowhere, we may realize that our minds were subconsciously solving a problem. If a resolution never reaches consciousness, we can't be certain if the mind was unable to resolve a problem, or if the mind ignored the problem entirely. That is why it is difficult to know if we are understanding information when we read silently without using language in conscious thought. We cannot be in touch with our subconscious to know what it is thinking about. Some readers doubt that they understand at all if they don't use language in conscious thought. If they don't hear an inner voice, they assume they are not thinking, or are not thinking well. In fact, language can be a helpful mediator, since it forces us to focus more fully on a specific problem. That is probably why some of us refuse to take the risk of trying to read silently without consciously thinking the words on the page and without consciously thinking about our personal reactions.

Third, readers tend to operate at the level which is most efficient. Effective readers automatically switch levels to find the one that is most appropriate at a given time. That is, readers may pause to think about a morpheme, word, sentence, paragraph, or chapter when they believe they have found vital information which contributes to a clear understanding of the text. We believe, however, that most uncertainty is resolved after words are read; that words are the most convenient and frequently-used units in reading. Reading centers on words, labels for concepts and the relationships among the concepts.

An argument needs to be made that supports the conclusion that words are the most convenient units to process in reading. First, however, we must define word. A word can be described at many levels. The semantic level is the most familiar. The semantic level concerns conceptual understanding. A word is a label for a generalization. A generalization describes the invariable characteristics of the members of a group of objects, ideas, and events. A word can be described morphemically, as a combination of fundamental units of meaning. The word boys, for example, can be described as a morpheme that refers to a young human male, and a morpheme that signifies plurality. A word can be described syntactically, for the role it plays in a sentence, such as noun, verb, adjective, adverb, and preposition. A word can be described phonologically as sound units within a term that are arranged sequentially according to the sound conventions in a particular language. A word can be described orthographically as a spelling pattern. For example, C-A-T represents many of the sounds we associate with the term cat. Spelling, however, does not indicate accent and pitch. A word can be described typographically as letters, ranging from one to many, sequentially spaced from left to right with uniform small spaces between the letters and uniform larger spaces at either end. In addition, a word can be typographically described as appearing in styles such gothic, roman, and italic.

Now let's continue the argument that supports the conclusion that words are the most convenient units to process in reading. Our first piece of evidence concerns the operation of vision. When eyes fixate, pause and focus, on the printed page, the mind only perceives a little of the signal that is brought to it. Each fixation is limited to approximately about ten spaces of print. Depending on the lengths of words, a single fixation may bring in two words and the space between them, parts of two words and the space in between, a word and the spaces surrounding it, parts of a single word, or some other combination. The amount of useful information perceived from each fixation will vary, but is limited. Since each fixation brings little useful information, and since no useful information is received in the brain when eyes move forward (a saccade) or backward (a regression) between fixations, readers' physical limitations force them to see letters in clusters that are near the lengths of single words.

Next, the typographical arrangement of words on a page encourages readers to look at individual words, not at uninterrupted strings of letters, or phrases. (ex., uninterruptedstringsofletters) It is convenient to look at words, since they are physically separated from each other. The importance of this segmentation is often underrated. Verbal language is spoken as a stream of sound that rarely stops and starts between words. We are deluded when we believe that words are segmented in speech. The speaker does not segment sounds into words; the listener does. This generalization can be demonstrated if you listen to someone speak in a language you do not know. You hear a steady stream of sound, not individual words. As people learn language, they learn to perceive segmentation from the stream of sound that they receive from their environments.

It is natural for people to hear, think, and speak in units that they believe are words. Words are the richest sources of information. The strong belief in the convenience and efficacy of words in verbal language probably accounts for the print convention which physically separates words. Words are meaningful in speech and print; individual phonemes and graphemes, or random combinations, are not. Reading centers on concepts that are represented by words, and on the relationships among the concepts that are detailed by words.

Given the operation of vision, typographical segmentation, and the rich, informational content of words; words are the most convenient units processed during reading.

So far, we have primarily shown you how generalizations are used to reduce phonological, typographical, orthographical, morphological, semantic, syntactic, and rhetorical uncertainty. Now we want to detail how generalizations, hypotheses, and evaluations are used to make sense of levels of meaning beyond that which is represented by a single word.

Example 1 will be used to show how an effective reader might use generalizations to make sense of a text.

____Example 1_____

A modern Yo-Yo is made of two discs connected at their center by an axle around which a string is tied. The string's free end is tied with a loop around a person's finger. After the string is wound around the axle, the Yo-Yo is dropped. It then spins out and back into the person's hand as the string unwinds and rewinds.

The Yo-Yo was first used as a primitive weapon fashioned from a sharp piece of flint-like rock, with a long thong tied to it made from the hide of an animal, or perhaps twisted from plant fiber. Hunters would hide in the leaves of trees and wait for prey to pass. When an animal or human enemy passed

Example 1, continued

underneath, the rock was thrown in an attempt to hit and stun. If the stone missed, hunters could retrieve their weapon without leaving the safety of their hiding place. If their aim was true, hunters jumped to the ground, wrapped the thong around the prey's neck, then strangled it.

During the centuries, the Yo-Yo developed from a crude weapon to a fascinating toy. The first recorded appearance of the Yo-Yo as a toy was in ancient Greece. There are several vases which show pictures of Grecian youths playing with Yo-Yos in the National Museum in Athens. An ancient terra cotta Yo-Yo which is delicately decorated with figures on a white background is also on display.

Countless generalizations can be reinforced or formed by making sense of the symbols in the text. Depending on interest and purpose, readers will determine what uncertainties they want to consider. The uncertainties may be dictated by teachers, or chosen independently by readers. A sample of the questions which could be asked about the Yo-Yo text, and their probable answers, are listed below. Note that all of the answers in this case are generalizations, but that is not always necessary. It is the case here, since the passage does not contain hypotheses or evaluations. Also note that the questions are asked in a sequence that corresponds to the order which is used to present introduction in the text. This approach facilitates understanding, but does not have to be followed. Questions could be asked in any order.

Q. What is the design of a modern Yo-Yo?
A. A Yo-Yo has two discs connected at their center by an axle around which a string is tied.
Q. How does a Yo-Yo operate?
A. After the string is wound around the axle, the Yo-Yo is dropped. It spins out and back into a person's hand as the string winds and rewinds.
Q. When was the Yo-Yo first used?
A. It was used in primitive times.
Q. How was the Yo-Yo first used?
A. People first used Yo-Yos to hunt.
Q. What is the procedure for using a Yo-Yo as a weapon?

A.   From a hiding place, a hunter throws the Yo-Yo in an attempt to stun the prey. If the throw is unsuccessful, the Yo-Yo is easily retrieved. If the throw is successful, the hunter strangles the prey with the string.

Q.   How did the use of the Yo-Yo change?

A.   The Yo-Yo was first used as a weapon, then it was used as a toy.

Q.   Where can ancient vases be found which show Grecian youths playing with Yo-Yos?

A.   These vases can be found in Athens at the National Museum.

Teachers and students could ask questions involving hypotheses and evaluations that are <u>inspired</u> by the Yo-Yo text. For example, the question "Why does a Yo-Yo move up and down?" could be asked. A pertinent answer might include information about gravity, balance, and the forces of action and reaction. The question "Why is a rifle a better weapon than a Yo-Yo?" could also be asked. A pertinent answer favoring a rifle might mention the advantages of speed, killing power, and safety. The information needed to answer these two questions, however, is <u>not</u> signalled by the text. Readers would have to rely on background knowledge to answer these questions. The questions, therefore, are tests of previous learning, <u>not</u> tests of a student's understanding of the author's message.

Now let's look at a text that presents an argument supporting a hypothesis by examining example 2.

___**Example 2**_____

A survey has shown that seven of ten people feel that they are impostors. They believe that they have fooled others into overestimating their abilities. They attribute their successes to luck, more than to ability. Most of all, they fear being discovered as impostors.

Pauline Chance, author of <u>The Impostor Phenomenon--Overcoming The Fear That Haunts Your Success</u>, believes that being in creative fields such as art or writing may result in feelings of being an imposter. The criteria for success in creative fields are subjective and can change quickly. It is difficult if people only judge themselves on their popularity. It is easier to define success and to maintain a healthy belief in oneself when objective, consistent criteria are applied

Example 2, continued

by the public.

Feeling like an impostor may also be caused by parents whose praise is too global. Parents may tell children that they are bright, but the children feel like impostors when they go to school and can't do everything easily and well. When a child receives a c in math, and a's in history, English, and chemistry, he (or she) may unrealistically feel that teachers in all areas will soon give him tasks that he won't be able to successfully complete and realize that his success was due to luck or lenient grading.

Being a perfectionist may also lead to feelings of being an impostor. People may feel that what they have accomplished has not been good enough, so they keep raising their expectations to unreasonable heights. They change the standards themselves.

Numerous questions could be asked about example 2 requiring that generalizations be used as answers. For example, the question "Who wrote The Impostor Phenomenon--Overcoming The Fear That Haunts Your Success?", would probably be answered with "Pauline Chance wrote the book.". Other generalizations are included in the list of sample answers provided below. We believe that the most crucial information in the passage, however, is the argument that changing public taste, global parental praise, and ever-increasing personal standards cause people to feel like impostors. The following questions and probable answers might be discussed to understand the argument.

Q. What is an impostor?
A. An impostor is a person who feels that he or she has fooled others into overestimating his/her abilities.
Q. What proportion of the population feels like an impostor?
A. Seven out of ten people feel like impostors.
Q. What is one piece of evidence which helps explain why people feel like impostors?
A. People in creative fields are affected by the frequently changing tastes of the public, since they often tie their feelings of self-esteem to their popularity.
Q. What is a second piece of evidence which helps explain why

	people feel like impostors?
A.	Parents whose praise is too global may lead children to believe that they should be capable of great success in every area. Children are confused when they experience difficulty. Their expectations are too high.
Q.	What is a third piece of evidence which helps explain why people feel like impostors?
A.	Perfectionists are often dissatisfied with their standards. They ultimately raise their standards to unrealistic heights in an effort to be perfect. They cannot be satisfied by the success they've earned.
Q.	What is the argument presented in the passage?
A.	Changing public taste, global praise from parents, and ever-increasing personal standards cause people to feel like impostors.

If we believe the evidence, then we can understand why people might feel like impostors. In this case, the effect can be caused by any one of three alternatives.

Now let's look at a text that presents an argument supporting an evaluation by examining example 3. Remember that an evaluation reflects an appraisal, a choice from among values. Remember too that generalizations and hypotheses are formed after objective evidence is considered, while evaluations are formed after subjective evidence and objective evidence are considered.

____**Example 3**_____

Theft is usually associated with stealing products or possessions from warehouses or houses. Stealing is contrary to American law, and it violates God's law, "Thou shalt not steal."

A computer software program is a valuable proprietary product. Software publishers estimate that millions of dollars in revenue are lost each year due to pirates who duplicate, use, and often sell unauthorized copies of commercial programs. Duplicating computer software without permission is a form of theft. As a result, manufacturers aggressively search for illegal operations and prosecute whenever possible. In addition, manufacturers are actively seeking effective methods for protecting their products from duplication.

Example 3, continued

Since theft in any form is unacceptable, and people who duplicate computer software without permission are thieves, then software pirates are behaving in an unacceptable manner.

The following questions and answers might be discussed in an effort to understand the argument.

Q.   What evaluative standards are mentioned?
A.   Social and religious justice, American law and God's law, are the standards mentioned which note the view that stealing is unacceptable.
Q.   Do people duplicate computer software without permission?
A.   Yes, people duplicate, use, and often sell unauthorized copies of commercial products.
Q.   What is the author's evaluation?
A.   The author believes that it is unacceptable to duplicate computer software without permission.
Q.   What argument does the author use?
A.   Since stealing is unacceptable, and people who duplicate software without permission are stealing, then people who duplicate software without permission are behaving in an unacceptable manner.

The argument in example 3 moved from a statement of the evaluative standards to a generalization that could be supported to the conclusion. This is the classic structure for an argument which supports an evaluation. It is not necessary, however, for the argument to be presented in this sequence. The argument could have been presented in reverse order, starting with the evaluation. The argument could have been presented in any possible combination, but an unconventional structure would make it more difficult to follow the argument.

We will conclude our discussion of the reading process with a special note. We purposely use the term understanding instead of comprehension throughout this textbook. We prefer understanding, since it places more emphasis on the readers' active role in reconstructing an author's message. Understanding ascribes respect to the efforts of readers. Active, conscientious, knowledgeable readers are needed to interpret an author's message by filtering symbols through their unique minds. We also prefer <u>understanding</u>, since it does not imply that the goal of reading is to stop after achieving a comprehensive, complete, perfect translation of the author's thinking. Effective readers do not stop thinking when an author's message is transposed. Active, effective readers move beyond the author's message by thinking divergently.

Conclusion

An examination of the rhetorical structure of this chapter noted by the headings and subheadings will reveal two main emphases. First, we described many of the variables which influence reading. The variables were placed in three categories: those that are related to readers, texts, and the environments in which reading occurs. We hope this discussion convinced you that reading is complex and fragile. Second, we described how effective readers process information. Essentially, readers make sense of printed materials in the same way that they make sense of other parts of their worlds, by reducing uncertainty through the use of generalizations, hypotheses, and evaluations.

Introduction to Chapter #3

Reading and writing are explorations which take us from wonder through mystery to knowledge. While reading, we follow a map that an author has charted for us. While writing, we chart a map for others, and personally benefit by discovering landmarks and courses that we were not aware of before. Writing helps us to clarify thought in awareness, and to benefit from our subconscious knowledge, as illustrated in the following quotation from Leonard Bernstein, famous composer and conductor.

> I was merely writing a symphony inspired by a poem and following the general form of that poem. Yet, when each section was finished, I discovered, upon rereading, detail after detail of programmatic relation to the poem--details that had 'written themselves' wholly unplanned and unconscious. Since I trust the unconscious implicitly, finding it a source of wisdom and the dictator of the condign in artistic matters, I am content to leave these details in the score.[1]

---

[1]Joan Peyser, <u>Bernstein</u>, (New York: Ballantine Books, 1987), p. 158.

Chapter 3

The Writing Process

Will the use of the printed medium be greatly reduced in the future? Will reading and writing be replaced by more efficient methods which will help humans cope with the demands that will be imposed by the continuing information explosion?

Information is a growing resource. William Baker, president of Bell Laboratories, has estimated that the amount of information in the record has doubled every seven years since the end of World War II. An indication of the immense task which Americans face in processing this information is provided by Baker's determination that "a weekday copy of The New York Times has as much to read as the educated individual in 16th-century Europe absorbed during his lifetime."[2] This information explosion is a self-sustaining monster, since the probability of new discoveries is enhanced as information increases. This, of course, is progress. The information explosion is also fed by improved methods for recording, storing, and disseminating information. Even if, in some instances, we aren't saying anything original or important, we're saying it to more people, more often.

How has our culture dealt with the information explosion? Some of the technologies that are available or will be available in the foreseeable future for recording, storing, and disseminating information include:

> --Microelectronics which improve the speed of computers and allow for the possibility of reducing an entire computer to the size of a postage stamp.

> --Computer-driven cathode ray tube printers capable of composing text of graphic arts quality at speeds up to 6,000 characters a second.

> --Microprinters, xerographic devices that preview microfilm images on a screen and enlarges them onto ordinary paper.

> --Advanced typesetting methods that can set composition for an

---

[2]N. R. Kleinfield, "Ma Bell's Great Dream Machine," New York Times, 28 May 1978, sec. 3, pp. 1,9.

entire encyclopedia in only a couple of days, and with as many different type faces and weights as are needed.

--Nationwide facsimile transmission services, capable of transmitting or receiving any printed or written material. Stations will eventually be located in airports, bus stations, hotels, and banks.

--Huge communications satellites, serving as relay stations for cross-country television broadcasting, phone service, data transmission, or any kind of wireless signals.

--Television newspapers which can broadcast the equivalent of a page of printed materials into the home every 10 seconds.

--Talking typewriters. These computers talk back, offering new facts, reinforcement, advice, and can print the words you speak into them.

--Individualized instruction available through home television sets with the capability of two-way communication.

--Low cost, three-dimensional color television communications services which will reduce the need for business travel.

--Fiber optics which transmit sound and computer signals transformed into laser beam impulses and are capable of carrying more signals with greater fidelity than wire.

--Accelerated speech devices which increase the speed of a recording without distorting the voice.

--Microfilm reduction techniques which can reduce all 1,245 pages of the Bible to a two-inch square of plastic.[3]

Will these achievements reduce the importance of print? No. It is essential to note that many of these methods of communication rely heavily on the medium of print. They rely on scripts; technical materials for the production, use, and repair of equipment; and frequently the product is intended to be read.

---

[3]Quentin Fiore, "The Future of the Book," Media and Methods 5 (December 1968):20-26.

In the immediate and foreseeable future, the use of the printed medium will probably increase. As a result, students must develop reading and writing abilities, so they are prepared to cope with the future.

Variables Which Influence Writing

Someone writes something for someone somewhere. Another way of stating that sentence is to say that an author writes a text for an audience within an environment. The following discussion of the variables which influence writing is an attempt to make our introductory statement more understandable.

Variables Associated With The Author. Authors must be human. Computers cannot think imaginatively. They can only manipulate information using programmed instructions. In addition, computers are dependent on humans for their existence and operation. It is doubtful that animals, other than humans, think imaginatively. Animals may act in amazing ways, but these actions are constrained by their instinctive programs. In addition, even though some animals can communicate through movement or speech, no animal has developed a symbolic writing system for communicating. Only human authors can produce imaginative, printed text on their own.

In the last chapter, we stated that reading requires physical stamina. Writing demands even more stamina than reading, since authors must not only think and see, but must coordinate muscle movements as they move a pen or push the keys of a typewriter or computer keyboard. Speed and legibility of writing are functions of stamina and eye-hand coordination; physical strength and physical dexterity. Fortunately, almost all secondary students have sufficient strength and coordination to handle writing without difficulty.

Emotion influences writing, since emotion influences all human activities. Emotion can be an aid or a detriment to writing. As an aid, it helps determine a purpose for writing. Writing serves the same purposes as reading: pleasure and knowledge. An author can write for personal enjoyment, or to entertain others. An author can write to learn, or to bring information to others.

Writing can satisfy personal needs for pleasure. For example, writing can help satisfy the needs of autonomy, achievement, and order. Autonomy involves the urges to exercise freedom of expression and to obtain financial independence. The right to have and state a belief is an assertion of self, while financial independence earned by selling texts increases experiential opportunities. Achievement involves the need to succeed and excel. An accomplishment is an affirmation of one's existence, a boost to self-esteem. The achievement may be the creation of a unique idea, a message which reflects that the author is a spiritual or intellectual frontiersman. The achievement may be the eloquence with which a writer expresses ideas. A proposition may not be original, but its statement may be aesthetically pleasing. Of course, the achievement could also be the attainment of membership in that cherished circle of published authors, who receive approval from editors, book sellers, and critics. Writing can satisfy the personal need for order; the desire to keep things in proper sequence, to make advance plans, or to arrange details of work, so that life runs smoothly.

Writing can please others. Printed materials can spiritually nurture an audience. For example, greeting cards, stories, plays, and poems can convey sympathy, appreciation, and love. Authors reach-out through their written works to increase the happiness of others.

The need to clarify and obtain new information can be satisfied by writing to learn. Conscientious authors may pause before or after a complete draft is produced to get constructive feedback. For example, authors may compare their notes or drafts to journals and books by other authors which contain relevant information to determine if their treatment is comprehensive. Authors can also learn by receiving feedback to their materials from audiences. Authors may learn as editors and colleagues respond to their materials. Finally, authors may learn by reflecting on and evaluating their own work. The printed page is a proving ground where authors test their ideas and the language that is used to express them. As authors interact with their own work, they can recognize gaps, inconsistencies, and awkward expressions. As authors interact with their own texts, they coax ideas out of the subconscious and into awareness. This technique for eliminating uncertainty may be the greatest benefit of writing. Writing can be used to offer knowledge to others. The desire to influence the thinking and actions of others can be conveniently satisfied through the powerful medium of print. Printed material can inform and persuade. Printed material can inform readers about traditional academic subjects such as history and biology. Printed material can inform readers of strategies for emotional and social growth; strategies for coping with anxieties people bring on themselves and with anxieties that are caused by others.

Emotion can also upset the writing process. First, low self-esteem can upset the process. Prospective authors may feel that they do not know anything that would be interesting or valuable for other people to read. Prospective authors may not have confidence in using language or unfamiliar rhetorical forms to express their ideas. These two attitudes may not be justified, but may be caused by low self-esteem. Second, prospective authors may not want to express their ideas for fear that someone else has already expressed similar ideas. Teachers have done their best to give students the impression that they are stealing ideas if the ideas are even remotely similar to anything anyone ever said in human history. It's impossible to know what numerous outside influences contributed to the development of a specific idea. It's hard to know how we became the people we are. Besides, no outside influences may have ever been involved. The idea may have originated in the imaginative mind of the student without a strong outside influence. In fact, very few ideas are absolutely new, without precedent. Readers should be thrilled when they find that a famous person had similar questions and answers, not heartbroken and dejected. Third, students may not want to complete a writing assignment, if it is uninteresting to them. Students may not work at all. Students may work half-heartedly. Students may not make all the revisions that are needed to put a work in a form that finally satisfies a teacher. No matter how much teachers cajole, students ultimately decide how much effort to expend. Fourth, prospective authors may believe that it is illicit to write for their exclusive satisfaction, or that they do not deserve to indulge in such luxury. In part, this may represent the conflict between writing to communicate and writing for the sake of art. Does writing have to have a purpose beyond itself, or is it enough that an aesthetically pleasing piece of art was created? Others are served in the former case, while only the creator is served in the latter case. Due to a belief that it is selfish to be self-indulgent, and perhaps due to low self-esteem, prospective authors may refuse to write for themselves. Others may forbid it, or the author may forbid it himself/herself.

In addition to physical and emotional condition, the mental condition of an author must be considered. Mental condition includes memory and background knowledge. When related to writing, memory refers to what the author has already expressed or the plans that were made for future inclusion; and background knowledge refers to the ideas an author might express and conventional patterns for expression. Memory rarely detracts from writing. If authors do not remember what they wrote, they can go back and read the convenient record they produced. If authors do not remember what their plans were for forthcoming sections, they can read what they've written and hope that the connections can be remembered that were made when the original passage was written, or they can refer to any notes that were made about topics, phrases, and sequence. Memory is not as important to writing as background knowledge. Background knowledge is crucial. Authors must have a message to communicate, or at least have the knowledge to create a message as they write. Authors must have generalizations, hypotheses, and evaluations to express as content. Authors must be familiar with various writing tools and materials. Authors also must know linguistic conventions regarding typography, orthography, semantics, syntax, and rhetoric.

In regard to tools and materials, authors must know the advantages and disadvantages of using common articles such as pencils, pens, typewriters, computers; paper, and video monitors. Some advantages and disadvantages are inherent in the tools and materials, while some depend on an author's personal preferences. For example, pencils and pens are readily available, inexpensive, portable, and simple to use. Pencil marks are easier to erase cleanly than ink marks from pens and typewriters, yet, since graphite is not as bold as ink and fades over time, it isn't preferred when making permanent records. Computerized word processors allow for the easiest and cleanest manipulation of text. Text can be changed on a video screen without the ponderous effort required to change text on paper. Authors do not have to rewrite and reorganize by cutting, pasting, taping, drawing arrows, writing in margins, scratching-out words and sentences; or reformat by completely retyping pages to accommodate minor changes when a computer monitor is used. Text can be produced quicker, if a person can type faster than write with a pencil or pen. More attention can be paid to meaning, since spelling and syntax programs can be used after a draft is completed to locate and correct problems. Of course, computerized word processors do have disadvantages. They are not readily available to every individual who may want to use one due to their relatively high cost. They are larger and more difficult to move than a pencil and a pad of paper, especially if a printer must accompany the computer. Finally, they require that a user be able to proficiently manipulate a keyboard, and remember numerous commands which vary depending on the software program.

Before mentioning specific linguistic conventions, it is important to describe what conventions are in general. Conventions are agreements about how people should act in certain circumstances. Conventions are accepted ways of doing things; customary practices. Many conventions are formalized in law, such as those stated in local, state and federal statutes. Other conventions are informal agreements made within a society. For example, there is a protocol for courteously introducing strangers. Conventions make life more convenient.

Writing is based on a social convention; the agreement that authors should attempt to signal their messages as clearly as possible. Good writing should be clear and appealing to authors and readers. This convenience makes life easier, less chaotic, less uncertain for everyone. Life moves quickly. Readers do not usually like to be inconvenienced and confused when they have to struggle through text that is written in a highly unconventional, overly complicated style. Authors and readers are pragmatic; they provide and seek answers in the most economical ways possible. Strunk and White nicely state the need for economy and clarity in writing in the following quotation.

> A sentence should contain no unnecessary words, a paragraph no unnecessary sentences, for the same reason that a drawing should have no unnecessary lines and a machine no unnecessary parts. This requires not that the writer make all his sentences short, or that he avoid all detail and treat his subjects only in outline, but that every word tell.[4]

Clarity is a conventional convenience. In addition, authors are expected to use linguistic conventions in their quest for clarity, appeal, and ease of reading. The linguistic conventions which authors are expected to use are basically the same as those which readers are expected to use. Writers and readers need to work within a linguistic system where conventions regarding typography, orthography, semantics, syntax, and rhetoric are understood and followed. Authors should make choices that readers would expect them to make.

Variables Associated With The Text. It is simple to separate a text from a reader. It is extremely difficult to separate a text from its author. A text is not a product of the reader, but it is the product of an author. A reader does not decide what symbols will appear on a page, but an author does. As a result, authors and their texts are intimately related. A discussion of the variables associated with texts could have been subsumed in the previous section which discussed the variables associated with authors.

In chapter #2, we described many of the linguistic generalizations which readers must know and use to make sense of texts. Typographical generalizations refer to print style, spacing, margins, direction (left-to-right and top-to-bottom in English), capitalization, and punctuation. Orthography refers to spelling patterns. Semantics concerns word meaning. Syntax concerns word order within sentences. Rhetorical generalizations concern the structure of paragraphs and the structure of forms such as poems, plays, and research reports. Since these are basically the same generalizations that authors use as they write, there is no need for us to say much more about them. We must, however, make one very important point about generalizations.

---

[4]William Strunk and E. B. White, The Elements of Style, (New York: The Macmillan Company, 1962), p. 17.

After examining generalizations at all levels, we conclude that all linguistic generalizations are conveniences. Remember that a society chooses its symbols, modifications, and referents. There is no irrefutable logic which compels a society to use b instead of the letter ~, the upper-case form B instead of the lower case form b only, the spelling cat instead of cta, the term cat instead of gato or meower, or chronological order instead of random order when presenting ideas. Conventions are made and used because they simplify communication. Conventions make it easier to make sense of the world.

The visual appearance of a text makes an important impression on readers. Visual appearance reveals clues to an author's self-respect and respect for the audience. Illegible handwriting, distractive marks, and irregular spacing may be due to time constraints. Authors may hurry to produce a text so their handwriting can keep up with their rate of thinking, or so they can meet an imminent deadline. Sometimes, however, materials that are difficult to decipher reflect low self-respect. Handwriting analysts believe that illegible handwriting can reflect an author's attempt to take-back a word or idea at the same time it is being expressed. Don't be quick to discount this phenomenon. Teachers often find that a student's handwriting suddenly becomes unreadable on an essay test when the student isn't sure of a spelling, the technical name for a specific concept, or the definition of a concept. Illegibility may help reduce the risk of criticism, the consequence of being wrong. Illegibility may also reflect a lack of respect for the audience. The author may not deeply care if an audience benefits intellectually or aesthetically from the work or not.

Attractive visual appearance increases the tremendous power of print to influence. People are apt to exclaim, "It's in print, so it must be true!" particularly when examining a newspaper, journal, or book that has been typeset. Material that is handwritten or obviously typed on a typewriter or low quality computer printer does not usually elicit the same response. It is likely that the power of typeset material can be attributed to at least two variables. First, readers often infer that editors and other authorities thoroughly scrutinized and approved the material before they allowed it to be printed at a relatively high expense and risk. Second, the visual impression made by neat typeset pages is one of permanence and importance. The pages look like they must be important because of the time and care that went into their production. Lawyers are required to have certain formal documents typeset. Businesses take advantage of visual image by having their annual reports to stockholders professionally printed. Alert students take advantage of visual appearance when they print their assignments on laser printers in the hope that teachers will subconsciously associate their work with the carefully produced works of confident, professional authors.

A final point needs to be mentioned. It is arbitrary and unnecessary to distinguish "creative writing" from other types of text, even though teachers often make such distinctions. Teachers try to distinguish between "creative writing" such as poems and fictional stories and less imaginative, more mundane compositions such as historical and laboratory reports. From a practical standpoint, we have not found an <u>ideal</u> definition which separates "creative writing" from "uncreative writing," or any absolute need for distinguishing between the two. From a philosophical standpoint, we believe that all writing is creative, since <u>all</u> thinking is creative and writing is an expression of thinking. In the end, it is a matter of degree, not difference.

Variables Associated With The Audience. Authors write for an audience. The audience may be restricted to the author alone, as when you write to help you clarify your own ideas in a draft, or when you express a private message in a confidential journal or diary. The audience may be identifiable as a particular teacher, peer, or parent; or as a particular group, such as Kiwanians, or scholars who are knowledgeable and interested in learning more about the Civil War. The potential audience may be so broad that it is undefinable, but authors must write with a specific audience in mind, since it is impossible to satisfy every possible reader.

A sense of audience helps an author determine what ideas and means of expression to choose. Authors should respond to the perceived characteristics of their audiences. One important characteristic pertains to purpose. If readers want to read to learn, then writers should choose content and a style that fit this purpose. Authors will write texts from which students can learn the information they seek. For example, if the audience will consist of high school sophomores who are enrolled in their first course in world history, an author will include the content he thinks students should learn, at a level which students can understand given their background knowledge, and in a form which suits their purpose.

An understanding of register is needed so an author can decide how to address an audience. Register refers to the tone and manner of expression. Register varies depending on the audience and the purpose for writing. When you write a personal letter to a friend describing current international events, you use different words, a different amount of detail, and a different level of formality than when you describe these events in a report that will be submitted to a teacher for a grade. When you write your parents for money, you use a different tone than when you write a silly poem to entertain them. Tone and expression vary when you write for parents, teachers, younger children; and when you write to demand, persuade, or move through emotion.

An understanding of register is especially important to people who use a dialect that is different from the standard followed by the majority culture in a society. If people wish to fully participate in and benefit from social, educational, and commercial opportunities, they need to have the flexibility to adjust register depending on the audience addressed. Educators refer to two types of register that are important to dialect speakers: home-talk and school-talk. Home-talk is the language that people use every day with their friends and families. School-talk is the more formal and standardized language that people are expected to use when presenting themselves to people who are in positions of authority, such as teachers, bankers, and university admission officers. School-talk uses the conventions that the majority culture expects. It is easier for people to assimilate into a culture when they satisfy language expectations.

Variables Associated With The Environment. Fewer than half of the 2,800 oral languages spoken on Earth have written forms. Societies which developed written forms felt a need for extending the usefulness of language. Reading and writing are sophisticated derivatives of the natural language processes of listening and speaking. However, due to their nature as secondary language forms, special care must be taken to ensure their development. Environments which encourage and support the development of reading and writing must be even more nurturing than those needed to develop listening and speaking. Listening and speaking develop naturally, but reading and writing generally are not learned without a high level of instruction.

Since a great amount of instruction is needed, all teachers must help by assuming responsibility for developing students' abilities to read and write. It is difficult, but essential, to convince teachers that they must be teachers of reading as well as teachers of specialized subjects. It is even more difficult, but equally as important, to convince teachers that they must be teachers of writing too. Literacy is not simply the domain of English teachers. Literate students gain more from their studies of history, chemistry, and calculus. The first step to developing healthy environments for nurturing literacy, therefore, is for teachers to dedicate themselves to creating rich environments in their classrooms.

What are the characteristics of environments which nurture the development of writing? A partial answer is provided by the following list.

--Low anxiety. An atmosphere exists where the consequences of being wrong are minimized. Students feel that their efforts will be respected. Students trust that their intimate thoughts will be understood and kept in confidence. Students are not afraid of being punished by low grades for presenting unusual ideas or using unconventional approaches.

--Valuable experiences. Rich environments provide numerous, interesting experiences which build knowledge; thereby giving students something to write about. In addition to knowledge, valuable experiences develop the skills of observation and reflection.

--Available models. Students are shown examples of good writing. The examples illustrate various forms (ex., research reports, sonnets, plays, persuasive essays, mysteries, autobiographies, short stories) and the individual styles of authors. Students are also shown early drafts of a finished work so they can see that good writing requires an author to polish writing through revisions. Often, teachers will share one of their writing efforts with students and discuss the reasons for changes made from revision to revision to convince students that good writing is rarely produced in an initial draft.

--Encouragement to read like writers. Students are usually encouraged to concentrate on the content of what they read. However, students read like writers when they concentrate on the content and on the conventions that authors use to express themselves.

--Functional activities. Students write to accomplish tasks that have functional purposes: tasks that directly enhance learning or communication. For example, students are more interested in recording the results of an experiment than in completing worksheets that they think are only given to keep them busy. Students do not spend time completing exercises that are unrelated to genuine communication, or exercises which are not assigned on the basis of individual need.

--Freedom of choice. Students are allowed to choose a writing activity to complete from a menu of related alternatives.

--Frequent opportunities. Students write often, since writing is the best way to learn to write.

--Adequate writing supplies. Students have an adequate supply of pencils, pens, typewriters, computers, paper, note cards, correction fluid, scissors, and tape.

--Sufficient time. Students have sufficient time to research topics, develop ideas, produce drafts, and edit. Sufficient time is crucial, since it is not always easy to quickly express what is known or felt. Teachers take the extra time that is needed to read and respond to what their students write.

--Different audiences. Students write for themselves, peers, parents, and adults outside of the school; not just for teachers, who are often the only audience students consider.

The remaining portion of this section on environmental variables will focus on feedback, a variable which contributes greatly to the nurturing of writing. Feedback is crucial as writing is encouraged and guided, since mere practice will not lead to improved writing. Helpful feedback is needed as any complex learning is undertaken, like learning how to write. Constructive feedback suggests improvements.

Teachers traditionally provide feedback to students by writing on and returning papers to individuals, or by sharing examples of difficulties and their resolutions with entire classes. The examples occasionally come from textbooks, but are more impressive if they are taken from the actual work of current students. Discussing real, immediate problems personalizes the feedback, and the problems are likely to be ones which other students will face in their writing. When using examples taken from the works of current students, however, it is important to save students from embarrassment by not revealing the names of the authors.

Teachers should not be the only respondents, particularly if they were not the intended audience. For example, students might write their principal to recommend steps that could be taken to conserve energy in the school building. The principal, as the intended audience, would be a better judge of the content and persuasiveness of the recommendations than the science teacher who gave the assignment. Peers can also provide feedback. A student author can be paired with a single peer or a group of peers who will respond to the author's composition. Group approaches can be very effective with secondary students. Students can learn about empathy, tact, and group dynamics. Authors can feel intense gratification from pleasing peers.

Students are extremely sensitive to feedback, especially if they perceive criticism in the tone. Students are so sensitive, that they will sense criticism despite respondents' protestations that their intentions are noble and their advice that feedback should not be taken personally. Most authors find it virtually impossible to separate themselves from their manuscripts, since writing is an intensely personal activity. Writing is more demanding and formal than speaking. Writing is more personal than reading, since it is more constructive than reconstructive. It takes a whole lifetime of experiences and a unique person to author a manuscript. Compositions do reflect their authors. A rejection of an author's writing is a rejection of the author. As a result, any response to a manuscript must be gentle. Respondents should not use red pencils as swords that slash and cut an author's heart. Manuscripts should not be made to look like blood-soaked battlefields.

Feedback should be provided when students are still interested in their work. Interest drops quickly if the work was only produced because it was required. Students must ultimately decide when they have completed their final revision. Teachers transfer feelings of ownership from students to themselves when they require that work be done to their satisfaction, instead of to the satisfaction of students.

Teachers and other respondents also transfer ownership to themselves when they impose changes on students, especially when the changes alter an author's ideas. Teachers should make specific suggestions for improvement, but allow students to decide which changes to adopt. Teachers should be particularly careful when suggesting changes in ideas, since students are more sensitive about such suggestions than straight-forward suggestions regarding punctuation, spelling, syntax, or word choice. Ideas are the heart of a work and should never be ignored. If response time is limited, respondents should at least respond to content, which is the most personal, human aspect of a composition. Authors learn about themselves through writing. Authors must be nurtured so they can grow. Effective nurturers are more concerned about clear ideas and stylish expression, about life, than about the presentation of neat, conventional squiggles on a page. Writing, like patterns of living, is nurtured, not taught.

Like life, more nurturing and guidance are needed at the beginning, with the ultimate goals being competence and independence. Teachers should strive to develop successful, independent authors. The best teachers make themselves obsolete as soon as possible.

A Description of the Writing Process

Writing is done by unique individuals for various purposes. As a result, it is not possible to detail a single description of the writing process. In an effort to help you understand the writing process, however, we will provide a general description of what effective writers do as they produce printed language symbols.

Like reading, writing is thinking. Writing is reasoning. Writing is a decision-making process. Writers use their knowledge of generalizations, hypotheses, and evaluations to express, learn, and communicate.

Writers must begin by deciding on a worthwhile purpose to accomplish. Authors ask, "How will I benefit from writing?" Writers may choose to write for enjoyment, entertainment, personal improvement, or to guide others. Writers must be highly enthusiastic about achieving their goals. Enthusiasm is even more important in writing than in listening, speaking, or reading; since writing is more difficult and demanding. Enthusiasm must be maintained for authors to persevere.

Once the commitment to write has been made, effective authors prepare by choosing a topic, identifying relevant ideas, recognizing an audience, organizing the ideas within a format, estimating the length of the composition, determining how much time to spend, and deciding on tools and materials. In this way, authors answer the questions, "What do I have to say to my audience?" and "How will I go about stating my ideas?" A general plan is formed.

The next logical questions for authors to ask are, "What important information do I need to find?" and "How will I find it?" Authors may need to research their topics by examining newspapers, magazines, professional journals, monographs, interviews, books, artifacts, research data, and reference materials. When authors feel they know enough to begin writing, they start their first drafts.

Writing is most intensive as authors create the first complete version of their compositions. Writing, like speaking, puts thoughts into awareness so ideas can be identified and clearly expressed. Ideas and means of expression are brought from subconsciousness to consciousness. We discover what we know, which leads to additional development. During writing, there is a continuous interplay between discovery, production, and development. Writing is a dynamic process in which what is written influences what will be written.

An author influences a page, and the page influences the author. This influence derives from meaning. Decisions regarding word choice, sentence structure, and paragraph length are driven by meaning, not by mechanical limitations as to an allowable number of words in a sentence, lines in a paragraph, or paragraphs in a chapter. Meaning-based decisions give authors control. Authors examine what they have written and ask, "Have I said what I wanted to say?" or in other words "Has my purpose been met by the words, syntactic patterns, cohesive devices, and transitional techniques I chose?"

The difference between writing and the examination of what was written is similar to cognition and metacognition as they were described in the chapter on reading. In reading, people think to reconstruct a message. In writing, people think to construct a message. In reading, people think metacognitively when they consider their thinking to determine what they learned and what they still need to learn. In writing, people think metacognitively when they consider their own writing to determine if they expressed themselves clearly, and if they need to add information. Metacognition allows for regulatory control.

Metacognitive thinking is more difficult to accomplish successfully when a person is an author instead of a reader. Metacognitive thinking requires that people distance themselves from their cognitive thinking. It is easier to separate oneself from another person's work in order to be objective, than to remove oneself from one's own work. Authors are close to their ideas. In part, that is why reviewers and editors suggest final revisions before a manuscript is published. Authors know what they intended to say, so they may read more into a manuscript than another person. What seems obvious to an author may be unclear to a reader. Feedback from an audience can be a powerful aid to an author's metacognitive thinking.

Authors rewrite as they write. All decisions made while writing are tentative. Some decisions are reaffirmed. Some decisions are immediately changed. Some decisions are changed after a considerable period has passed. A secret to successful writing is to spend little attention on revision when words are first being put on paper. Too much attention to neat penmanship, correct spelling, helpful punctuation, or precise word choice detracts from the flow of ideas. The goal to keep in mind during the initial writing is the fluent expression of thought, rather than recopying or proofreading. Authors should write quickly so their attention and memory are not overloaded with chunks of information that are less meaningful. Effective writers concentrate on composition instead of transcription in two ways. First, authors may choose to ignore imperfections in penmanship, spelling, word choice, or organization during an initial drafting, intending to make modifications later. Second, authors who are proficient can revise so quickly that the flow of ideas remains relatively uninterrupted. Their reactions are practically automatic.

Most revision is undertaken after an author has completed a first draft. Revision is easiest when a complete picture is seen. It is easier to change and rearrange parts when the whole is seen. An author asks, "Have I stated my thoughts comprehensively and clearly?" and "How can I improve my writing to make a greater impression on my audience?" During the final editing, authors eliminate unimportant and redundant parts, smooth transitions, correct spelling and punctuation, add crucial ideas or examples, and improve word choice by substituting more active verbs, colorful adjectives and adverbs, and precise nouns for weaker choices.

Finally, the finished draft is neatly rewritten or retyped and presented to the intended audience. Presentation is crucial. If a manuscript is not given to the intended audience, the task seems incomplete and artificial. Unfortunately, teachers often frustrate students when they refuse to submit manuscripts to audiences, or when they require students to write for imaginary audiences. Students must feel that their efforts will accomplish real, worthwhile purposes. This does not necessarily mean that students must receive responses from their audiences, but that the possibility of response is not removed.

Writing, like thinking, is a meaning-seeking activity, an adaptive pursuit, a decision-making process that helps us make sense of the world. The world, in writing, is the knowledge in our heads; knowledge about ideas, strategies for developing ideas, and conventional techniques of expression. Authors reduce uncertainties, solve mysteries, about ideas and means of expression. Authors think, manipulate ideas, and develop ideas as they put printed language symbols on paper or screen.

Generalizations, hypotheses, and evaluations are important when content is being considered. Generalizations and evaluations are primarily important when expression is considered. As we stated earlier in this chapter typographical, orthographical, semantic, syntactic, and rhetorical generalizations are used in writing. Linguistic generalizations are used when people listen, speak, read, and write. Evaluations are made whenever authors judge the comparative worth of alternatives. Authors evaluate at every level of the writing process. Authors evaluate when they decide between topics, ideas, organizational patterns, spellings, punctuations, word choices, and syntactic patterns. Authors ask, "Which alternative has the greatest worth?"

Let's examine an example of evaluation at the word level. An author may look at the sentence "The horse walked on the trail," and sense that walked isn't the best choice that could be selected. The author would consider the intended meaning, alternative words such as <u>saunter</u>, <u>trot</u>, <u>canter</u>, and <u>gallop</u>; and would choose the word that best indicates the intended meaning. Since the author in this case wishes to refer to the horse's fastest gait, the word <u>gallop</u> is chosen. Remember that the evaluative standards of evidential truth, personal truth, aesthetic beauty, social justice, and religious justice may be used to judge value. <u>Gallop</u> has evidential value, since consultation with an authority or a dictionary would show that <u>gallop</u> is the accepted word for a horse's full-speed gait. <u>Gallop</u> is personally satisfying for the author, since he/she prefers to be precise and clear in writing. <u>Gallop</u> may also appeal to the author's taste. The author may like the sound or appearance of the word and prefer to use it instead of another alternative word, or instead of rewriting the sentence as in, for example, "The horse moved on the trail at full-speed." Precision and clarity are also aesthetic virtues associated with good writing. Writing is better art, more attractive, when it is precise and clear. Social virtues are fulfilled since communication with an audience would be enhanced by conventional, accurate word choice. Effective communication may even please a transcendental power, at least if the notion of transcendental power includes a belief that it is good to enjoy, entertain, learn, and teach. Arguments could be formed which support the choice of <u>gallop</u> that are based on truth, beauty, and/or justice.

The example in the preceding paragraph was not meant to imply that every decision is made after such thorough consideration, or that authors are always consciously aware of their decision-making processes. The example was intended to illustrate how effective decision making might occur.

Now that you have been given an overall description of how decisions are made at all levels of the writing process, it is time to concentrate on one specific aspect: the particular attention that is given to sentences. We will try to convince you that effective writers find it most convenient to concentrate at the sentence level, just as we tried to convince you that effective readers most frequently concentrate at the word level. This is not to imply that levels of meaning above sentences in writing or words in reading are not important. It is simply that authors and readers operate at convenient levels so they can move to higher levels of meaning as quickly as possible. Authors and readers act expediently.

To begin, we must define <u>sentence</u>. A sentence can be described typographically as a series of words that begins with a capital letter and ends with a concluding punctuation mark such as a period, question mark, or exclamation point. A sentence can be defined syntactically as a sequence of words arranged in a conventional order that is smaller than a larger structure such as a paragraph. These definitions, however, are not sufficient. Provision for meaning must be added.   As a result, we add that a sentence normally has a subject and a predicate. Every sentence normally has at least one combination of a subject and a predicate; such a combination is called a clause, but a sentence may have more than one clause. The subject is the word or word group that tells who or what performs or undergoes the action named by the verb or experiences the condition named. The predicate is the word or word group that normally follows the subject and tells what it does, has, or is, what is done to it, or where it is. A sentence can express a question, command, generalization, hypothesis, or evaluation.

How much meaning should be expressed in a sentence? Some authorities believe that a sentence should end when a complete thought is expressed. It is difficult to work with this standard, however. Consider the following sentence which expresses one complete thought: "Sue and I swam in the river on Tuesday after I read a blue book with 500 pages on insects in the library where the temperature was warmer than in Miami as reported by a television weatherman, certified by the United States Meteorological Society, who wore a brown three-piece suit while pointing to maps of North America." It is better to think of sentences as being adequate, rather than complete. An adequate sentence fulfills an author's purpose for that series of words. Authors end a sentence when it tells what they wanted it to say. A command explicitly states what should be done. A clear question determines the nature of an answer. A generalization adequately describes. A hypothesis thoroughly explains. An evaluation explicitly judges. An argument details evidence and a conclusion. Authors try to express thoughts accurately, clearly, and elegantly so that audiences will not be confused.

Now we can continue the argument which supports the convenience of attention to sentences. The first piece of evidence concerns meaning. Logicians believe that propositional meaning is only stated in declarative sentences which note generalizations, hypotheses, or evaluations. Logicians do not consider commands and questions when they examine meaning, since commands and questions do not assert relationships between ideas. Declarative sentences lie at the heart of meaning. A concept is described when it is compared and contrasted to other concepts. Likewise, the meaning of a printed term is described by other terms which relate to it. A sentence focuses on a subject, a concept that is described by the predicate. When authors say what they want about a subject in a sentence, they either state something different about the same subject in the next sentence, or move to a related subject. Sentences are fundamental units of meaning in writing and are linked to each other by meaning. Meaning is expressed effectively if one sentence smoothly leads to the next. Smooth transitions are signs that there are no gaps in meaning.

A second piece of evidence concerns memory. Authors have to remember ideas and terms of expression as they write. The length of individual sentences probably reflects the limits of human memory. Longer sentences include more meaning. If an author attempted to write an extremely long sentence, he/she would likely forget what was said at the beginning before the end were reached. Extremely long sentences also place a memory burden on readers. Authors who respect their readers will write sentences of manageable length. Given the limits on immediate memory, it can also be concluded that authors do not think about more than one sentence at a time. One subject and its predicate are about all that can be held in immediate memory. Authors do not consciously think about two sentences simultaneously.

A final piece of evidence which supports the convenience of attending to sentences concerns typography. Sentences are physically distinguished in print by certain conventions of capitalization, spacing, and punctuation. These conventions serve as landmarks which separate sentences from words, one another, and paragraphs. Since there are no logically compelling reasons which necessitate the use of these conventions, it can be assumed that the segmentation of sentences has served a purpose which is worth preserving. We believe that segmentation serves as an aid to writers and readers by delineating important chunks of meaning.

Given the rich meaningfulness of sentences, limitations to immediate memory, and typographical segmentation; sentences are the most convenient units to attend to while writing.

Conclusion

Authors make sense of the world and present their conclusions to audiences to accomplish meaningful purposes. Authors develop, express, and evaluate ideas by using conventions of language that they learn by listening and reading.

Writing is the most sophisticated and demanding language process. As a result, effective writing must take place in a nurturing environment where it is encouraged and guided, particularly when it is first being practiced.

Introduction to Chapter #4

This chapter describes strategies which students can use to organize, record, retain, reproduce, and locate information. Study strategies give students greater control over their thinking, reading, and writing. As students gain control over their own learning, they become more educated, and thus, more independent. Students should eventually be able to learn by themselves. As William Feather notes,

> An education isn't how much you've committed to memory, or even how much you know. It's being able to differentiate between what you do know and what you don't. It's knowing where to go to find out what you need to know; and it's knowing how to use the information you get.[1]

---

[1]William Feather, quoted in Quotable Quotes in Education, ed. August Kerber (Detroit: Wayne State University Press, 1968), p. 17.

Chapter 4

Study Strategies

Students need to use a structured approach when they study. That is, they must plan to make decisions which will allow them to gain the most from their efforts. In the description of the reading process in chapter #2, we noted that effective readers develop a plan for identifying, organizing, and remembering relevant information which varies depending on the reader's purpose and characteristics of the text. Numerous attempts to codify study strategies have led to an onslaught of acronyms such as EVOKER, SQ3R, PQ4R, SQRQCQ, PRST, PANORAMA, and REAP. SQ3R, for example, recommends that readers of social science and natural science Survey titles, headings, introductory paragraphs, summaries, and graphic aids to get a general idea of the information and to begin to create a framework for organizing the content. Next, readers should formulate Questions which they wish to have answered. These questions set the purpose for reading. The third step is for readers to carefully Read to answer the questions they formulated and take notes if they desire. Next, readers Recite the answers to their questions without referring to the text or any notes. This is intended to be a check of understanding and a first step in putting information into long term memory. Finally, readers Review the information by rereading portions of the text or notes in an effort to retain the information better.[2]

EVOKER was devised for use with prose, poetry, and drama. Students are supposed to Explore by silently reading the entire text, note unfamiliar Vocabulary words and seek their definitions, read the text Orally, locate Key ideas, Evaluate the quality of the author's writing, and Recapitulate by rereading the text.[3]

SQRQCQ was created to help students answer story problems in math. Students Survey by quickly reading the problem, Question to determine the specific nature of the problem, Read the problem carefully, Question to determine what operations must be performed and in what order, Complete by doing the calculations, and Question the accuracy of the calculations and the reasonableness

---

[2]Francis Robinson, Effective Study, (New York: Harper and Row, 1961), chapter 2.

[3]Walter Pauk, "On Scholarship: Advice to High School Students," The Reading Teacher 17 (November 1963):73-78.

of the answer.[4]

It must be noted that good students do not necessarily use specific study strategies such as SQ3R or SQRQCQ, that slow students cannot afford to spend the extra time studying that rigid adherence to these strategies requires, and that training in the use of these study strategies does not automatically transfer to real assignments. Despite these weaknesses, it is recommended that study strategies be discussed with students to emphasize the helpfulness of using a structured approach to study and to suggest steps that might be included in an individual's approach. Students should not be forced to follow specific study strategies in a rigid, unalterable manner. Successful students economize by doing only what is necessary for them to satisfy their purposes. Successful students develop individualized approaches. Successful students make good decisions.

Flexible Reading Rates

It is possible to reach a high level of understanding by reading quickly or slowly. Effective readers adjust their reading rates between and within texts to find the most efficient speed, while less effective readers tend to read everything at about the same pace. Flexibility is beneficial, since it allows readers to achieve an acceptable level of understanding as quickly as possible.

The variables that affect rate include purpose for reading, prior under-standing of the content, and the difficulty of the material in relation to reading ability. As we speak about rate and purpose in this section, we will not refer to purpose as related to pleasure or knowledge as we did in earlier chapters. Rate is not determined as much by the differences between reading for pleasure and reading for knowledge as it is by the type of information sought. If readers intend to locate a limited piece of information, they may scan. Scanning is a fast rate of reading. For example, a student may scan the periodic table of elements to locate the atomic weight of gold. The reader moves to the pertinent information as quickly as possible by using cues about the format of the table to separate the irrelevant from the relevant. Concentration is often aided when readers repeat the target information in their minds as they conduct their search to continuously remind themselves of their objective. If readers intend to gain a general idea of the content of a text, they may skim. Skimming is a rapid rate

---

[4]Leo Fay, "Reading-Study Skills: Math and Science," in Reading and Inquiry, ed. J. Allen Figurel (Newark, Del.: International Reading Association, 1965), pp. 93-94.

of reading. For example, a reader may skim a paragraph or chapter to determine what information it contains. The reader quickly samples the paragraph or chapter to determine if the information deserves more careful attention at a later time. Readers skim to identify the subject, evidence, or conclusion in a passage. If readers intend to wring as much meaning or enjoyment as possible out of a text, they will read carefully at a relatively slow rate.

Rate of reading is influenced by background knowledge. The more a reader knows about related information, the easier it will be to understand the information in a passage at hand. For example, an expert on the Civil War would be able to read an introductory text on the subject rapidly, since content would be readily anticipated and quickly verified. Prior knowledge is central to understanding and reading rate.

Rate is also related to reading ability. A reader's prior knowledge includes knowledge of language, as well as knowledge of content. Readers can recognize words and rhetorical structures faster if they are familiar with the visual appearance of words, conventional syntactic patterns, and conventional rhetorical structures through experience. Reading rate is increased when readers spend less time on recognizing printed symbols and the relationships among them, and more time on meaning. More attention is spent on understanding when symbols are recognized automatically.

At this point, it would be logical for you to ask, "How fast could a person read under the most favorable conditions?" This question can be addressed in two ways. First, we can examine physiological limitations. Discounting possible regressions, reflection time, distractions, and the time it takes for the eyes to move during saccades, a crude estimate can be calculated. Given data concerning the frequency, duration, and usefulness of fixations, a reader who is familiar with the information and the language in a passage can process the text at a rate between 550 and 600 words per minute. Eyes cannot move faster. The second way of addressing the question of potential reading speed is to ignore the assumption that reading entails the identification of every symbol on a page. It is necessary to believe that people can read successfully without seeing every symbol to account for the fact that people have understood information at high levels after being clocked at rates which exceeded 600 words per minute. Readers who exceed 600 words per minute are sampling from the page. What is the highest possible rate, given a definition of reading which does not require that every symbol be seen, but which does require that a high level of understanding be achieved? Unfortunately, the answer to this question is based more on myth than evidence. It is difficult to answer the question given the complexities of the interactions among purpose, background knowledge, and reading ability. We can only conclude that the upper limit of rate varies considerably, depending on the reader and the task.

During the 1950's and 1960's, educators were keenly interested in training students to read faster through the use of machines. Tachistoscopes, controlled readers, shadowscopes, and special films were rushed into schools, surrounded by an aura of technology, modernity, and behavioral psychology. Despite the promises of slick salesmen and overly enthusiastic consultants, the benefits of mechanical training were disappointing. Even when students learned to read faster while maintaining high levels of understanding, the benefits did not last very long. Students quickly returned to their old habits, particularly when their training had been conducted with materials that were different from the materials assigned in typical classrooms. The failure of these methods was due to the mistaken notion that efficient eye movement caused good reading. The reverse seems to be true; good reading causes good eye movement. The mind controls the eyes, the eyes do not control the mind.

The little value derived from mechanical training was due to its ability to influence motivation and attention. Students responded favorably to mechanical equipment, since it was novel and enthusiastically used by teachers. Interest was high, as it is in many classrooms today when computers are first introduced to students. Students also benefitted, because mechanical aids taught students to focus attention. Increased attention to print lead to faster processing.

If mechanical aids increased motivation and attention, two valuable benefits, why are these machines absent from school today or collecting dust in forgotten closets? The answer is that educators found that the same benefits could be accrued without elaborate apparatus. Teachers found that they could help students increase motivation, attention, and rate through sound instructional methodology. Teachers can help students by choosing interesting reading selections, developing needed content and language knowledge before asking students to read, setting a purpose for reading, assuring students that rate can be increased without a loss of understanding, suggesting various rates to be used at different places within a text, reminding students to concentrate, and by encouraging reading on a broad variety of subjects.

Organizing and Recording Information

Students need to know how to organize and record important information that they obtain from reading or from listening to oral presentations. Notes help students check their understanding of information, and provide concise sources that are useful for review. Because notes are so important, it is surprising that very few schools formally include instruction in note-taking in their curriculums.

One common technique for organizing and recording information in a book is to underline or highlight essential passages. The chief advantage of this technique is that it saves time, since the reader does not have to rewrite essential information. Of course, this technique can only be used when the reader has permission to write in a book. The technique works well if a reader readily recognizes an author's organizational plans within and among paragraphs. Underlined or highlighted passages serve as landmarks when readers retrace their steps through a text. When teaching students to underline or highlight, teachers should encourage students to read complete sections between headings or entire chapters once before making any marks on the pages. This allows readers to concentrate on the overall meaning of a section that is complete enough to stand alone. Readers should feel the sense of closure that the author intended, before reviewing and analyzing the parts of the whole. After reading a unitary chunk of material, students should reread with an eye toward marking essential parts. If two readings are completed, the potential conflict between reading to understand and reading to record can be avoided. It is easier to mark your path, after you know where you are going.

When an author's overall organizational plan is not immediately obvious, it may be necessary to outline a large section between headings or a chapter. An outline notes superordination and subordination of meaning in sequential order. That is, the structure of an outline indicates the relative importance of ideas in the same order as the author presents them. Constructing an outline helps students uncover an author's organizational plan. Example #1 illustrates the general structure of an outline.

____**Example 1**_____

Title

I.   Important idea
       A. Detail supporting I
       B. Detail supporting I
           1. Detail supporting B
           2. Detail supporting B
              a. Detail supporting 2

Example 1, continued

          b. Detail supporting 2
    C. Detail supporting I
II.   Important idea
    A. Detail supporting II
    B. Detail supporting II

There are two types of outlines: sentence and topic. Each point in a sentence outline is a complete sentence, while each point in a topic outline is a term or phrase. Teachers should ask students to construct sentence outlines before topic outlines, since the former are easier because the student can repeat an author's words. Students must take a second step when they create topic outlines. Students must use their own words to state an author's ideas in condensed form.

Modeling and feedback can be effective aids when underlining and outlining are being taught. Students should read a short, text, and then be shown the markings of a effective underliner or the product of an effective outliner. In this way, students can see an exemplary model. Next, students should read a text and make their own markings or outlines. The teacher then provides feedback by having a discussion which compares the students' responses to a model or to each other. Teachers can eventually wean students from a reliance on models by providing them with partially completed outlines which require that students provide more and more information from practice to practice. Ultimately, the students should be able to underline and outline successfully and independently.

Summaries can also be used to organize and record information. A summary restates an author's message in concise form. After reading an entire selection, students write the key generalizations, hypotheses, evaluations, and supporting details in their own words. Summary writing has two main advantages. First, summaries, unlike outlines, do not have to present ideas in the same order in which they appear in the text. Students are free to rearrange the order of ideas in an effort to make the message more understandable. Second, summaries take less time to produce than outlines, since they are less comprehensive. Good summaries only need to include the information which students feel is most pertinent.

Information can be organized and recorded when a student creates a structured array. A structured array summarizes information from a text by using lines and placement to show the relationships among terms. Example 2 contains a structured array which summaries information taken from a chapter in a biology text.

___**Example 2**_____

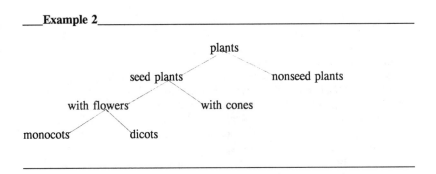

As you will see in chapter #5, teachers may construct a structured arrays to present to students before reading to give students a overview of the important information that will appear in the text. This builds background knowledge, helps set purpose, and models the format of a structured array so students understand how their own arrays should look.

It is more difficult for students to take notes from an oral presentation than from a text. Students cannot control the flow of words when they listen as they can when they read. They cannot regress to clarify ideas unless they ask speakers to repeat themselves, or unless they rewind and review a tape or film. They cannot pause to reflect, write annotations, or rehearse without running the risk of missing important input. Unfortunately, too, the typical classroom lecture is not as formally organized as a text, or a film. As a result, it is more difficult for students to understand how ideas are organized, and their confusion slows note-taking. Even so, a large portion of every school day is spent listening to lectures, from which notes could be taken.

Note-writing physically involves students, which helps them attend and learn. A good set of notes reveals a presenter's organization and accurately records important information. Notes can be reorganized, condensed, and reviewed before examinations. Because of its necessity and advantages, students should be carefully taught to take good notes.

Students should try to study a topic before a lecture on it is heard so they can gain the most from the presentation and write notes efficiently. Students can prepare for the lecture by completing assigned readings and activities on schedule and by reviewing previous notes.

During the lecture, students should concentrate and reflect before writing. It is necessary to sort and evaluate ideas before writing, since it is extremely difficult for students to write at a rate that keeps pace with speech. To save effort, students should omit anecdotes or detailed examples if the key idea is understood, use consistent abbreviations, and use shorthand if they are proficient in its use. Other suggestions can be made to students regarding missed information and personal reactions. Space should be left if important information is missed to remind the student to obtain the information at a later time. If there is time or a great desire to make personal reactions, they should be placed in the margins or in brackets to keep them separate from the ideas of the lecturer. This is particularly important in those unfortunate, but frequent, circumstances where lecturers expect students to limit themselves to parroting the lecturer's ideas, and the lecturer's ideas only, on examinations.

The basic teaching method of modeling and feedback which we recommended for teaching underlining and outlining can be used to teach note-taking. After giving a short lecture, a teacher can show students what a good set of notes pertaining to the lecture might look like. Next, the teacher can have students write their own notes during a second short lecture. When the presentation is finished, the students should discuss how their notes compare to a model. If teachers wish to challenge students, they can give additional practices to teach underlining and note-taking which begin with longer texts or lectures.

Retention

Memory has been discussed in previous chapters of this book, due to its importance in application and learning. Memory is required so people can understand the world and increase their knowledge. Memory will be discussed from a pragmatic perspective in this section, since students know that memory helps them demonstrate the knowledge they have learned through study when they complete examinations.

The development of memory aids, mnemonic devices, is an old and fascinating activity. You have probably used mnemonic devices to remember information such as the number of days in each month ("Thirty days hath September..."), the colors of the visible spectrum (ROY G. BIV= red, orange, yellow, green, blue, indigo, violet), the lines and spaces of the treble clef (Every Good Boy Does Fine, FACE), and correct spelling (The ending of the word that refers to the head of the school is p-a-l, since "The principal is your pal."). Mnemonic devices help us remember because they elaborate information. Elaboration involves the construction of meaningful relations between new information and preexisting knowledge. When we elaborate, we are actively involved in learning by consciously attending to the verbal and visual association of new information with old, familiar information.

The loci method requires that you associate new information with familiar places (loci). If you wish to memorize a list of terms or events, you can take an imaginary walk through a familiar location, associating each item on the list with a place. After rehearsing the associations, you will remember the items whenever you mentally retrace your steps. This technique was popular with Roman orators who used it to remember the key ideas in their speeches. For example, you are familiar with the layout of your house. If you enter the front door and walk clockwise around the house, you will move from the hall to the living room, to the dining room, to the kitchen, to the family room. Now let's associate the rooms in your house with the sequence of steps for starting the engine of a car with an automatic transmission which may have been explained in your driver education course. You were told to insert the key, make sure the transmission is in "park," push and release the gas pedal with your right foot, move your right foot to the brake and depress it, and then turn the key. Since you were just learning and couldn't remember the sequence automatically, you had to consciously attend to each step in turn. You may have aided memory by associating each step with a location in your house. You may have thought and visualized, "I 'insert' myself into the hall. In the living room, I 'park' myself on a chair. The things I eat in the dining room give me 'gas.' The kitchen 'depresses' me. My sister and I take turns 'turning' to television shows in the family room." If you wanted to increase the visual impact of the images, you might have imagined a person frantically rushing in the hall, a person with an enormous fanny in a chair, a person rubbing a stomach the size of a beach ball, a person crying in the kitchen, and two people having a tug-of-war with a copy of TV Guide. Retrace your steps through the house now to see if you remember the procedure for starting a car!

The pegword technique is a mnemonic device that is especially helpful for remembering items in a sequence. With the pegword technique, you can retrieve an item at any point in the series or review the series in a forward or backward direction. Numbers are paired with common words that rhyme with them. For example, 1--fun, 2--shoe, 3--tree, 4--door, and 5--strive. Once you know these pairs, any list of new items can be associated with the pegwords by using imagery. The words serve as pegs on which items can be "hung." Let's pretend that you want to run errands in a particular order so you can save gasoline. You want to get cash from the ready-teller, buy a Milli Vanilli album, see what merchandise is on sale at a discount store, get a flea collar for your cat, and celebrate your latest grade report by eating a triple-chocolate fudge-brownie sundae. You might think, "It is fun to say the word kiosk which can refer to the ready-teller building. A shoe is comfortable and so is good music. A tree stands tall, like the pole that supports the flasher for the blue-light specials at K-Mart. A revolving door and a flea collar are circular. The last few letters in StrIVE are similar to the letters in ICE." Your matched pairs are fun--kiosk, shoe--music, tree--pole, door--collar, and strive--ice. Since the number-pegword combinations do not change, you would be able to ask, "What is the third errand I will run?" and answer, "tree--pole, check the sale items at the discount store." The pegword technique is particularly helpful when you need to remember abstract terms. Abstract terms are harder to remember than concrete terms because their referents are not as tangible. Pairing an new abstract term with a standard, concrete pegword makes the abstract term easier to recall.

The keyword technique aids in the memorization of terms in a foreign language. Meaning is added through elaboration when you match a foreign term with a keyword in English. Matches can be made on the basis of sound, appearance, and/or meaning. For example, picadores is a Spanish word that refers to people who anger bulls during a bull fight by poking them with spears. A student studying Spanish may relate the term to the English term pick; since the first syllable in each is pronounced the same, the first few letters are the same, and there is similarity in meaning between "picking-at" and poking a bull. To recall the Spanish word a student may think, "The word I know that is like pick and is Spanish for people who anger bulls with spears is picadores." Visual imagery can be used to increase elaboration further, if the student tries to picture a pick in the "mind's eye."

Teachers should encourage students to use mnemonic devices, since they are easy to use, beneficial, and enjoyable. In fact, enjoyment increases benefit. It is easier to remember associations that are ridiculous and humorous. In addition, students should be encouraged to create their own associations, not rely on ones given to them, so that they are actively and deeply involved in their own learning. A person will remember associations easier, if the associations were made by the individual.

In addition to introducing mnemonic devices, teachers should describe the potential benefits of other approaches to memorization. First, spaced practice, rather than massed practice, should be used. Students usually remember better if they study for short periods that are spread over an extended time (spaced practice), instead of trying to cram large amounts of information into memory all at once (massed practice). In other words, students shouldn't wait to try to memorize everything the night before a test. Second, overlearning aids memory. The more students review and rehearse information, the easier it will be for them to retrieve it from memory. They should rehearse even after they are first able to recall information. Third, information is usually more meaningful if it is presented as an integrated whole before being presented in pieces. Bits of information are easier to remember if students know how the pieces fit into a larger picture; how the information contributes to the overall structure or development of an idea.

Preparing for Examinations

The prospect of taking an examination raises the anxiety level of most students, and raises the anxiety level of conscientious students the most. Anxiety stimulates students and can be beneficial. Too much anxiety, however, debilitates students. It prevents them from performing at their best. Students should be taught to control anxiety so they can adjust their mood to a level which excites but does not overwhelm. We believe that it is unfortunate that teachers and counselors rarely teach students to cope with anxiety, whether the anxiety relates to examinations or other aspects of life. As a result, we will begin this section on preparing for examinations by discussing a technique which can reduce test anxiety, but which can also be applied to other threats which life presents.

Wolpe and Lazarus developed a technique for reducing anxiety that has been successfully applied to a wide variety of anxiety-causing situations.[5] The technique will not help every person with every problem, but we recommend it for your consideration.

The first step is for the individual to learn to relax, since relaxation is the antithesis of anxiety. A person who is in a state of deep relaxation is free from the tension that accompanies anxiety. Any method which leads to deep relaxation can be used. Wolpe and Lazarus recommend a method that uses specific muscle-

---

[5]Joseph Wolpe and Arnold Lazarus, Behavior Therapy Techniques, (New York: Pergamon Press, 1968).

relaxing exercises. Example 3 contains a script to be recorded on an audiotape that guides you through the exercises.

___**Example 3**_____

General Relaxation Instructions

Begin by getting as comfortable as you can. Settle back comfortably. Just try to let go of all the tension in your body. Now take a deep breath. Breathe right in and hold it (five second pause). And now exhale. Just let the air out quite automatically and feel a calmer feeling beginning to develop. Now just carry on breathing normally and just concentrate on feeling heavy all over in a pleasant way. Study your own body heaviness. This should give you a calm and reassuring feeling all over (ten second pause). Now let us work on tension and relaxation contrasts. Try to tense every muscle in your body. Every muscle: your jaws, tighten your eyes, your shoulder muscles, your arms, chest, back, stomach, legs, every part just tensing and tensing. Feel the tension all over your body--tighter and tighter--tensing everywhere, and now let it go, just stop tensing and relax. Try to feel this wave of calm that comes over you as you stop tensing like that. A definite wave of calm (ten second pause).

Now I want you to notice the contrast between the slight tensions that are there when your eyes are open and the disappearance of these surface tensions as you close your eyes. So while relaxing the rest of your body, just open your eyes and feel the surface tensions which will disappear when you close your eyes. Now close your eyes and feel the greater degree of relaxation with your eyes closed (ten second pause). All right, let us get back to the breathing. Keep your eyes closed and take in a deep, deep breath and hold it. Now relax the rest of your body as well as you can and notice the tension from holding your breath. Study the tension. Now let out your breath and notice the deepening relaxation-- just go with it, beautifully relaxing now. Breathe normally and just feel the relaxation flowing into your forehead and scalp. Think of each part as I call it out--just relaxing--just letting go, easing up, eyes and nose, facial muscles. You might feel a tingling sensation as the relaxation flows in. You might have a warm sensation. Whatever you feel, I want you to notice it and enjoy it to the full as the relaxation now spreads beautifully into the face, into the lips, jaws, tongue, and mouth so that your lips are slightly parted as the jaw muscles relax further and further. The throat and neck relaxing (five second pause), shoulders and upper back relaxing, further and further, feel the relaxation flowing into your arms, elbows, wrists, hands and down to the very tips of your fingers (five

Example 3, continued

second pause).　Feel the relaxation in your chest as you breathe regularly and easily.　The relaxation spreads even under your armpits and down your sides, right into the stomach area.　The relaxation becomes more and more obvious as you do nothing but just give way to the pleasant serene emotions which fill you as you let go more and more.　Feel the relaxation--stomach and lower back all the way through in a warm, penetrating, wavy calm and down your hips, buttocks, and thighs to the very, very tips of your toes.　The waves of relaxation just travel down your calves to your ankles and toes.　Feel relaxed from head to toe.　Each time you practice this you should find a deeper level of relaxation being achieved--a deeper serenity and calm, a good calm feeling.

Now to increase the feelings of relaxation at this point, what I want you to do is just keep on relaxing and each time you exhale, each time you breathe out for the next minute, I want you to think the word relax to yourself.　Just think the word relax as you breathe out.　Now just do that for the next minute (one minute pause).　Okay, just feel the deeper feeling of relaxation.　To even further increase the benefits, I want you to feel the emotional calm, those tranquil and serene feelings which tend to cover you all over, inside and out, a feeling of safe security, a calm indifference--these are the feelings that relaxation will enable you to capture more and more effectively each time you practice a relaxation sequence.　Relaxation will let you arrive at a feeling of quiet inner confidence--a good feeling about yourself (five second pause).　Now once more feel the heavy sensations that accompany relaxation as your muscles switch off so that you feel in good contact with your environment, nicely together, the heavy good feeling of feeling yourself calm and secure and very, very tranquil and serene.

Now we can deepen the relaxation still further by just using some very special stimulus words.　Let's use the words calm and serene.　What I would like you to do is to think these words to yourself twenty times or so.　Don't bother to count.　Approximately twenty or thirty times just say to yourself "calm and serene" and then feel the deepening--ever, ever deepening--waves of relaxation as you feel so much more calm and serene.　Now you do just that; take your time, think of the words and feel the sensations over and over (pause one minute).　Good.

Now I am going to count backward from 10 to 1.　At the count of 5, I would like you to open your eyes, and then by the time I reach 1, just kind of stretch and yawn and then you can switch off the recorder and just go back and relax on your own.　Okay, now counting backward" 10, 9, 8, 7, 6, 5, open your

Example 3, continued

eyes, 4, 3, 2, and 1. Now just stretch and kind of yawn and then slowly get up and switch off the recorder and then you can go back and carry on relaxing as long as you wish.

The instructions in example 3 may have reminded you of activities that you have participated in before. The procedure is similar to hypnosis, meditation, guided imagery, and other techniques. The similarity between this and so many other techniques suggests that many people are able to relax by using this type of activity.

After knowing how to relax, students need to be able to determine their anxiety hierarchy. Sample events leading to and including the taking of a test are listed in reverse chronological order in example 4. Students can add any anxiety-producing events to the list, or delete any events that do not disturb them. First, a student must rank the events in order of decreasing anxiety. The student will put 1 next to the event that produces the most anxiety, 2 next to the second most anxiety-producing event, and so forth. Once the events have been put in rank order, the student uses a scale of 0 to 100 (0=complete relaxation, 100=the most anxiety producing situation an individual can imagine, such as falling out of a window) to determine the precise degree of anxiety produced by each event. After scale values are assigned, the list of events is rearranged with the least anxiety-producing event at the bottom of the list and the greatest anxiety-producing event at the top.

___**Example 4**_____

Rank Order	Scale (0-100)	Event	Completed Hierarchy
__	__	During the last 10 minutes of the test	_____
__	__	When you come to a questions you cannot answer	_____
__	__	Seeing the exam paper lying face down before you	_____

Example 4, continued

__ __	Awaiting distribution of the test	_____
__ __	On the way to school on the day of the exam	_____
__ __	The night before the exam	_____
__ __	The day before the exam	_____
__ __	Two days before the exam	_____
__ __	One week before the exam	_____
__ __	Two weeks before the exam	_____
__ __	One month before the exam	_____
__ __	_____	_____
__ __	_____	_____
__ __	_____	_____

Once students know how to relax and have determined their hierarchy of anxiety-producing events, they are ready to complete the process. The student relaxes. While maintaining deep relaxation, the student visualizes each anxiety-producing event, beginning with the least threatening event in the hierarchy. The mental images will evoke the feelings of the real scene. Eventually, it is hoped that the student will be able to maintain complete relaxation even when imagining the event at the top of the hierarchy, and will be able to transfer this feeling of calm to the actual event when it occurs. Relaxation becomes associated with the event. The occurrence of the event should trigger relaxation.

The reduction of anxiety is one step in preparing for an examination. Other steps include review and anticipation. Review entails the reinspection of readings and notes with the intention of clarifying and retaining information. Students review important descriptions, explanations, and judgments; seek clarifying information from their texts, notes, peers, or teachers when necessary; and rehearse the information to place it in long term memory.

Anticipation entails the prediction of test questions. It is easy for students to anticipate specific test questions when teachers describe the items beforehand, or when students are assured that the items will directly relate to explicit learning objectives that were presented before instruction began. It is difficult for students to anticipate test questions when they have to try to read a teacher's mind. Teachers who make learning objectives mysterious do a disservice to students.

Education is simplest when a teacher tells students what to learn, facilitates their learning, and tests to see if they learned what was expected.

Anticipation also entails the prediction of the techniques that will be needed to successfully complete an examination due to its format. Some educators refer to test-wiseness to describe knowledge about the science and art of taking tests. Knowing information and being able to reproduce it on an examination in a form that is acceptable to an examiner are two different abilities.

To be "test-wise" when taking an essay examination, students need to realize that penmanship, spelling, and neatness subtly influence evaluation, even when such things are not supposed to be part of the grade. When first receiving the test, students should relax, read the directions carefully, preview the questions, determine the weight of each question in relation to the overall grade, and plan a rough schedule for using their time most productively. Students should also know how to respond to specific words that are likely to be found in questions. Example 5 lists key words that are found on essay examinations, along with conventional responses.

Example 5

Describe	detail, define
Compare	note similarities
Contrast	note differences
Explain	account for, state reasons or cause
Evaluate	assign worth
List	enumerate with little or no elaboration
Prove	argue by presenting evidence and a conclusion

Multiple-choice tests need to be approached differently from essay tests. Multiple-choice tests are generally easier for students, since they only need to recognize correct answers, they do not have to construct answers. To make students test-wise about multiple-choice tests, students should be instructed to eliminate as many choices as possible before selecting an answer to a question, ignore illusory response patterns; guess, unless there is a special penalty for incorrect answers; and check their work. It is usually best to use a pencil to complete a multiple-choice test, since it is easy to erase pencil marks when an answer is changed. Pencils must be used to mark answer sheets that will be scored by machine. Of course, almost all secondary students will know that they must make complete erasures, and must not "bend, fold, mutilate, or spindle" answer sheets.

When taking a matching test students should ask if any item has more than one response, count to see if there is an equal number of items and responses, match responses to items that they are certain fit together (note: Some students find it easier to work from the items to the responses.), match responses to items that they think might fit together, and check their work. It is usually best to use a pencil to complete a matching test, since it is easy to erase pencil marks when an answer is changed.

When taking a completion test, students should ask if the length of the line to be written on within a sentence is a clue to the answer.

When taking a true-false test, students should consider each word carefully. An answer often depends on the explicit understanding of a key word. Words like always and never are used in extreme statements that are frequently false. Words like might and could are used in moderate statements that are frequently true. When in serious doubt, the student should flip a coin. (That is not a flippant remark.) Consistent reliance on probability will yield correct answers approximately half the time on a well-constructed test.

Conducting Research

One of the best teaching techniques is to allow students to research topics of their choosing and to write papers about their findings. This technique actively involves students in thinking, reading, and writing; exposes students to broader, richer resources than a subject area teacher and a standard classroom textbook, and develops literacy abilities which are needed to live independent, fruitful lives.

In Libraries. It is vital that students learn to conduct research in libraries, yet most secondary students are given insufficient instruction and practice. Students should begin by taking orientation tours of their school library and local public libraries. These tours familiarize students with library etiquette, borrowing procedures, layouts and personnel. It is important to know where sources can be found, and who can help in locating sources. Introductions to personnel should not be overlooked during tours, since librarians are fonts of helpful information.

When students are ready to start systematically researching a subject, they should begin by examining reference books such as encyclopedias, bibliographies, dictionaries, almanacs, and atlases. Students can identify pertinent reference works by consulting with the reference librarian, exploring the card catalog, and examining guides to reference books. The finest references to reference books are <u>Reference Books: A Brief Guide</u> and <u>Guide to Reference Books</u>.

Encyclopedias are helpful, since they offer broad overviews of subjects, cross references, and occasional leads to specific books and articles through bibliographic citations. Another advantage of encyclopedias is that their content can be accessed easily by students who understand alphabetical order and the use of indexes. General encyclopedias like the <u>Encyclopedia Britannica</u> and <u>Encyclopedia Americana</u> contain brief, easily understood entries. More detailed information can be found in specialized references such as the <u>McGraw-Hill Encyclopedia of Science and Technology</u>, <u>Encyclopedia of World Art</u>, <u>International Encyclopedia of the Social Sciences</u>, <u>Current Biography</u>, and <u>An Encyclopedia of World History</u>.

Like encyclopedias, general and specialized dictionaries are available. The <u>Oxford English Dictionary</u> and <u>Webster's Ninth New Collegiate Dictionary</u> are examples of general dictionaries, whereas the <u>Mathematics Dictionary</u>, <u>Dictionary of Economics and Business</u>, and <u>Harvard Dictionary of Music</u> are examples of specialized dictionaries. Specialized dictionaries describe terms in greater depth than general dictionaries. Dictionaries are more difficult to use than encyclopedias, so teachers should fully prepare students by teaching them the knowledge that is needed to gain the most from dictionaries. Students need to know how to use alphabetical order, guide words, phonetic alphabets, and abbreviations for parts of speech. In addition, students need to know that word forms (ex. great: greater, greatest), etymological information, usage conventions, and definitions may be found in individual entries; and that appendixes containing valuable information on a variety of subjects may be attached at the end of the book.

Almanacs, books of quotations, and atlases may also offer pertinent information to a student's research. <u>Farmers' Almanac</u>, <u>Statistical Abstract of the United States</u>, <u>World Almanac</u>, <u>Bartlett's Quotations</u>, <u>The New Book of Unusual Quotations</u>, <u>World Book Atlas</u> and <u>Columbia-Lippincott Gazetteer</u> are popular references that are found in many libraries. Almanacs and books of quotations require that students be able to use a table of contents and an index. Atlases require that students understand scales, directional indicators, abbreviations, symbols, color coding, latitude, and longitude.

After examining reference books, the next step in library research is to locate books which may contain additional information about the subject. Potentially helpful books can be identified by examining sources such as Cumulative Book Index and Subject Guide to Books in Print. The titles of potentially helpful books must be checked against a library's computerized catalog or card catalog to see which books are on the shelves, since no single library contains every book that has been printed. Computerized catalogs are beginning to appear in greater number in libraries and seem to be the wave of the future. Instructions for using computerized catalogs vary, but are usually easy to follow. The instructions normally appear near the terminals and tell the user how to call up the basic information that has traditionally been included in card catalogs: title, author, and subject indexes. Often, students will start with a library's subject index to identify books about a subject instead of beginning with a broader source such as the Subject Guide to Books in Print. This approach is practical, but not comprehensive.

When a book listing is found, either through a computerized or card catalog, the listing will include a call number. The call number tells how a book is categorized. The call number and a library map help the student locate the book in the library. The call number may be taken from one of two systems: the Dewey Decimal System, or the Library of Congress Classification. General subject areas are signified with numbers in the Dewey system and with letters in the Library of Congress system. Each of these general areas is broken into subdivisions, but only the general subject areas are shown in example 6.

___**Example 6**_____

Dewey Decimal System

000-099	Reference books. These books usually have <u>R</u> on the spine and can rarely be taken out of the library.
100-199	Philosophy, psychology, and ethics
200-299	Religion and mythology
300-399	Social Sciences; such as law, government, education, vocations, civics, and economics
400-499	Languages
500-599	Sciences; such as mathematics, physics, chemistry, biology, zoology, and botany
600-699	Useful arts; such as medicine, engineering, agriculture, aviation, and manufacturing
700-799	Fine arts; such as painting, music, photography, and recreation
800-899	Literature; including poetry, plays, novels, and literary criticism

Example 6, continued

900-999 History, geography, travel, and biography

Library of Congress Classification
A	General works
B	Philosophy--religion
C	History--auxiliary sciences
D	History and topography (except American)
E & F	America
G	Geography--anthropology
H	Social science
J	Political science
K	Law
L	Education
M	Music
N	Fine Arts
P	Language and literature
Q	Science
R	Medicine
S	Agriculture--plant and animal industry
T	Technology
U	Military service
V	Naval service
Z	Bibliography and library science

Students need a great deal of generic knowledge to profit from the books they locate. Students must how to benefit from a title page, table of contents, preface, map, graph, table, diagram, illustration, photograph, footnote, bibliography, glossary, appendix, and index.

After locating books, students need to locate articles that appear in magazines, newspapers, and professional periodicals. The Reader's Guide to Periodical Literature contains author and subject indexes to articles of interest to the general public which were published in over a hundred magazines. The New York Times Index is an excellent guide to articles which have appeared in one of America's greatest newspapers. Community libraries often have indexes for reputable, local newspapers. The Social Sciences Index, MLA International

Bibliography, Humanities Index, and General Science Index are examples of specialized guides to articles in professional periodicals.

Once bibliographic information is found about pertinent articles, the student can try to locate a copy of each of the articles. Students should not be surprised if popular or professional periodicals are not locally available. There are so many magazines, newspapers, and professional periodicals that no library can afford to purchase or try to store them all. To check whether a library holds a particular periodical, students need to request a "periodical list," sometimes called a "serials list." This is a listing of the periodicals that the library has in its collection. If the article is in a publication that is less than a year old, the publication will probably be found loose on shelves in a special reading area for periodicals. If the periodical is older, it may be in a bound volume with a call number on a shelf like a book, or it may be on microfilm or microfiche in a special viewing room. The periodical list will indicate how location varies depending on age.

Students need to take notes to record the results of their research. Notes help students synthesize, remember, and organize information taken from diverse sources. Students need to develop their own style for taking notes. Teachers need only suggest that notes contain the bibliographic information which is required by the format (ex., American Psychological Association, Modern Language Association) selected, that quotations be clearly separated from paraphrases, that quotations be accurate, and that personal comments be kept separate from the author's views.

Most library research involves books and periodicals, yet other resources are available too. Libraries keep collections of artifacts, photographs, slides, films, phonograph records, audiotapes, videotapes, and models that might be helpful to researchers. Students must be made aware of these valuable resources, and taught to use them.

The availability and formats of the books and periodicals used in research varies tremendously. As a result, teachers should prepare students to use what is available in the school and community libraries, instead of describing materials that students may never use. Commercially prepared instructional programs that teach research skills may have to be modified to match local resources. In addition, commercially prepared exercises must be blended into meaningful, functional classroom assignments. The materials should not be used in isolation. They should become part of the solution to a learning problem. Students are bored by exercises that seem pointless. The exercises should yield results that advance a research project.

Through Interviews. Most of the research which students conduct is completed in libraries. That is why we described library research at the beginning of this section. We would like to turn now, however, to an exciting research technique that we would like teachers and students to use more often: interviewing. An interview is a good way of securing information; especially information about the experiences of people who have colorful histories, interesting hobbies, or responsibility for planning the future. Interview candidates are not hard to find, and are usually extremely flattered by an invitation to participate. Candidates can include school leaders, teachers, administrators, parents, community leaders, and people who have interesting occupations. An interview also gives the interviewer practice in courtesy, thinking, speaking, and listening.

After getting a candidate to agree to an interview, the student needs to prepare, schedule, and conduct the interview. Preparation requires that students plan the questions they will ask and conduct research so that the interview focuses on information that is not obtainable from a written record. Time is wasted and interviewees are insulted, if students ask questions which could have been eliminated through advance preparation. Scheduling requires that a time and place be found that are convenient for both parties. It may also be helpful to give the candidate a list of questions so answers can be considered before the interview. Candidates who are not used to being interviewed particularly appreciate this thoughtfulness.

When the interview is conducted, students might wish to use standard techniques. Good interviewers establish rapport by introducing themselves, restating their purpose, and thanking the interviewee for his/her participation, and asking permission for an audio recording to be made. Audio recording frightens some interviewees, so they should be allowed to decide whether a machine is used or not. Good interviewers let the interviewee do most of the talking during the interview. The interviewer should only intrude to ask a new question or to have the interviewee expound further on a subject. The interviewer should take careful notes, especially if the interviewee might be directly quoted later. The interviewer should thank the interviewee for his/her helpfulness to end the interview.

After the interview, students should be encouraged to review their tape or notes to clarify their thoughts while the interview is fresh in their minds. If possible, confusion should be eliminated by recontacting and asking the interviewee for clarification. When a transcript or a report about the interview is completed, it is polite to send a copy to the interviewee with a note of appreciation.

Time Management

It is difficult for secondary students to arrange their time so they can read, review, research, and write. In fact, it is more difficult for them to plan in advance than for university students. University students are usually given most or all of their assignments at the beginning of a term. Secondary students are often surprised during the course of a term by receiving assignments that are due on short notice. Secondary students are often heard to scream such things as, "But that means I'll have two tests tomorrow!" and "I can't do that this week, because of the big history paper I'm writing!" In addition, secondary students are not always successful at estimating how much time it will take to complete an independent project like a research paper, because of their relative inexperience.

As students receive assignments, they need to adjust their schedules. Students need to consider an assignment's deadline, the time it will take to complete the assignment; time demands made by jobs, recreational and service activities, and other school assignments; and the priorities which they attach to the tasks. Some assignments receive high priority because they are interesting, are given by a favorite teacher, or will be weighted more when a final grade is calculated.

Teachers can help students manage time by encouraging them to keep calendars on which they plan by the day or week. Teachers can also help by announcing assignments well in advance of their due dates, by setting interim deadlines for the submission of parts of projects, and by being generous when estimating how much time students will have to spend to complete projects to the teachers' specifications.

As a rule of thumb, teachers should set a deadline after estimating how long it would take a slow student to complete the task. As time increases, so does the probability of success. Taking a simple example, a textbook chapter of 50 single-spaced pages may take approximately 1 hour to read by a student reading at a rate of 400 words per minute, and 2 hours by a student who reads at 200 words per minute. This example does not account for distraction, deep reflection, fatigue, and is probably too generous in assuming that fast and slow readers could understand a moderately difficult text at such high rates. It is more realistic to assume that moderately difficult material will be read at approximately

200 and 100 words per minute, increasing the time needed to complete the reading to 2 hours for a faster reader and 4 hours for a slower reader. Using the slower, but also realistic, rates of 100 and 50 words per minute, the time needed would increase to 4 hours and 8 hours respectively. Differences among students are dramatic and should not be underestimated. The slowest and the quickest students will appreciate the luxury of time.

Introduction to Chapter #5

A fictional teacher in Kahlil Gibran's <u>The Prophet</u> commented on teaching:

> ...And he said: No man can reveal to you aught but that which already lies half asleep in the dawning of your knowledge.
>
> The teacher who walks in the shadow of the temple, among his followers, gives not of his wisdom but rather of his faith and his lovingness.
>
> If he is indeed wise he does not bid you enter the house of his wisdom, but rather leads you to the threshold of your own mind.
>
> The astronomer may speak to you of his understanding of space, but he cannot give you his understanding.
>
> The musician may sing to you of the rhythm which is in all space, but he cannot give you the ear which arrests the rhythm nor the voice that echoes it.
>
> And he who is versed in the science of numbers can tell of the regions of weight and measure, but he cannot conduct you thither.
>
> For the vision of one man lends not its wings to another man...[1]

Teachers cannot ensure learning, despite their best efforts, since learning depends primarily on the efforts of active learners. Yet, effective teachers realize that they can facilitate learning by establishing conditions which encourage learning. This chapter will describe techniques that will help teachers make wise decisions as they create healthy learning environments.

---

[1] Kahlil Gibran, <u>The Prophet</u>, (New York: Knopf, 1973), pp. 56-57.

Chapter 5

Making Decisions About Instruction

Learning and teaching are decision-making processes. You have already read how people learn by making decisions that help them make sense of their worlds. In this section, you will see that teachers make decisions that help them make sense of that part of the world that deals with instructional tasks. Teachers make numerous decisions as they decide why it is important to introduce a topic, how to present information, and how to evaluate learning.

One of the first decisions that teachers make is to select a general strategy for making decisions about instruction. Teachers use such a strategy as a metacognitive device. That is, teachers use the strategy to organize instruction by thinking about teaching. Teachers normally find it helpful to obtain diagnostic information, establish goals, select facilities and materials, choose procedures, and formulate a plan for measurement and evaluation. This strategy is described on the following pages and is reflected in daily lesson plans, such as the examples presented in this chapter.

Obtaining Diagnostic Information

Teachers must begin instructional planning by obtaining diagnostic information. Three types of diagnostic information might be obtained: information about a student's need to learn the content in question, a student's interest in the content, and a student's knowledge of the content.

Teachers begin to gather information about a student's need to learn by examining a school district's curriculum guide. This information helps a teacher prioritize potential learning objectives. School districts publish curriculum guides that detail the conclusions which students should understand. Curriculum guides describe what students are expected to learn in a particular year, course, or program. Teachers are required to concentrate on these prescribed expectations, although they are free to enrich the curriculum.

The interests of students can be investigated through discussions or questionnaires. Teaching is easier when students are interested in what a teacher chooses to teach, but such a correspondence does not always occur. If teachers become aware that students are not interested in achieving required objectives, then the teachers must take special care when motivating students. Of course, if a majority of students are not interested in learning non-required information, the teacher should plan to teach something else.

Pretests can be given to measure a student's knowledge of the content in question and related ideas. Teachers should determine whether students are already familiar with the evidence that will be presented. If they do not understand the evidence, they will not be able to form a valid conclusion. Also, teachers should determine whether the students already understand the conclusion in question. It is a waste of time to present an unnecessary lesson.

A teacher may use the same test before instruction that will be used to measure learning after the lesson is completed. Such an approach focuses learning since it familiarizes students with the anticipated outcomes of learning. Students do not have to guess the teacher's expectations. Learning is increased when the mystery that surrounds learning goals is decreased. In addition, pretesting informs students of their strengths and weaknesses so they know what personal resources they have which could be used to overcome their deficiencies.

Establishing Goals

The second step in instructional planning is to establish goals. Teachers should clearly specify what is to be accomplished and by whom. The goal can be for an individual or a group. Goals are sometimes called "learning objectives" or "behavioral objectives." After determining the current status of student knowledge during diagnosis, the goal is established to indicate what the teacher wants the student to know after instruction.

Selecting Facilities and Materials

The third step in planning is to choose facilities and materials. Instruction can occur in a classroom, laboratory, theater, forest, meadow, stadium, or museum. Instruction can be given at a zoo, circus, or farm.

Two sets of materials need to be chosen: materials that the teacher will use, and materials that the students will use. A teacher may use textbooks, trade books, newspaper articles, lists of questions, photographs, illustrations, graphs, movies, slides, filmstrips, transparencies, projectors, opaque machines, and concrete examples such as spheres, musical instruments, chemical compounds, and historical artifacts. Students may use sheets of paper, pens, workbooks, dittoes, laboratory equipment, musical instruments, animals, dictionaries, encyclopedias, thesauruses, mathematical tables, periodic tables, and calculators.

Reading material is commonly used as a teaching tool. As a result, teachers try to ensure that students have the reading ability to process the text.

Unfortunately, it is difficult to match students and texts because of the difficulties in measuring reading achievement and textual difficulty. Standardized tests of reading achievement are given infrequently to secondary school students, so their results may be two to three years old by the time a teacher sees them. In addition, standardized tests of reading achievement can be criticized because they confound understanding and memory, create high levels of anxiety, waste precious instructional time and limited financial resources, and yield scores that are derived from an extremely small sample of reading tasks. Most importantly, scores from standardized tests do not reflect the level at which students can recognize words and understand during normal classroom instruction. Standardized tests are intended to compare a student's score with a group's performance and are more useful to administrators than teachers. Standardized tests are not designed to produce the precise diagnostic information about a student's reading level that is needed by classroom teachers.

It is also problematic to determine the difficulty of reading material. Numerous statistical formulas, called readability formulas, have been developed in an effort to estimate the difficulty of printed passages by examining linguistic variables. Word frequency and sentence length are the linguistic variables that are most commonly examined by readability formulas, since readers tend to have difficulty reading words that appear infrequently in print, and in reading complex, lengthy sentences. Readability formulas, however, have not been highly successful. Readability formulas do not consider variables related to an author's style or organization. For example, the classic The Picture of Dorian Gray by Oscar Wilde has a readability of fourth grade as calculated with the Fry Readability Graph. It would be unwise to use the book with fourth grade students, however, since variables such as thematic sophistication, figurative language, and symbolism would make the book too difficult for the typical fourth grade student to understand.

Most importantly, readability formulas do not consider the reader. Difficulty is determined more by a reader than by print. A word in isolation like "xenophobia," for example, cannot be assigned an accurate level of difficulty. Difficulty is determined in the mind of a reader. It is a person who decides if a word is easy or hard to name or understand. A person who is familiar with cultures and travel may not have any trouble with the word "xenophobia." Yet, readability formulas do not examine a reader's background or interests.

Since standardized tests and readability formulas are seriously flawed, how might teachers match students and books? It is reasonable to have students interact with a particular text to see if their background knowledge is sufficient to process the material. Two ways of having students interact with a text have been suggested. The first method is the cloze technique. A passage of at least 250 words is taken from the text in question. The passage should have a clear beginning, middle, and end so that it offers sufficient ideational continuity. The first and last sentences are not altered, but every fifth word is deleted in each of the rest of the sentences. A line of uniform length is substituted for each of the deleted words so that length does not serve as a cue for the missing word. Students are told to read the passage and fill-in the missing words. When each response is scored, only the exact words that the author used are accepted as correct. Semantically appropriate substitutes (ex., "car" for "automobile") are not considered correct. If students' responses are correct 44-57 percent of the time, the material is considered to be at their instructional level. That is, the material is appropriate for classroom instruction since the students understand most of it and seem capable of understanding all of it with guidance from a teacher. If students score higher than 57 percent correct, the material is considered to be at their independent level. In other words, they are capable of understanding nearly all of the material without help. If students are correct less than 44 percent of the time, the material is at their frustration level. At the frustration level, students are overwhelmed by the difficulty of the material and probably won't understand it, even if a teacher tries to help them read it. The cloze technique is a valid approach for determining readability. Some teachers are cautious about the technique, however, for three important reasons. First, the sample passage may not be representative of the average difficulty of the textbook. The passage may be easier or more difficult than the textbook as a whole. Second, a 250-word passage is only a small reading sample. Scores may not be entirely reliable, since they are based on a single sample. Third, cloze passages create high anxiety among students, especially the better readers who are conscientious and sensitive. Scores on cloze tasks tend to be low. Students do not usually feel that they are doing well as they complete a cloze task. Even when students get slightly more than 57 percent correct when their responses are checked and are told that they are successful independent readers, they realize that they still only got slightly more than half correct and are not pleased. Students also dislike the idea that semantically appropriate synonyms cannot be counted as correct answers. Students feel they are unfairly treated, even when teachers explain that the acceptance of synonyms would violate the conditions under which the criteria for evaluating cloze passages were established.

A second method of having students interact with a text is to use a reading inventory based on passages taken from a particular textbook. Procedures for constructing and using reading inventories vary from authority to authority. For example, the number of passages to be read and their lengths vary. However, it is common for authorities to suggest that five passages of approximately 250 words each be used. A set of questions which is intended to check understanding is prepared for each passage. Students are instructed to read each passage silently and record their answers to the questions. A total score in the 75-90 percent range indicates that the material is likely at a student's instructional level. A total score greater than 90 percent indicates that the material is likely at a student's independent level. A total score less than 50 percent shows that the material is at a student's frustration level. A total score between 50 and 75 percent leaves a generous span for doubt. Reading inventories have been criticized since their passages may not be representative of the difficulty of the entire textbook, 1,250 words is a relatively small sample of reading performance, and the criteria for determining levels is not impeccably precise. Nevertheless, reading inventories present students with tasks that are most like their regular classroom reading activities. As a result, students are less threatened by this approach than by the cloze technique. Reading inventories are best used when teachers are in the midst of selecting a textbook for purchase in their school. It is wiser to test a book for its helpfulness before it is bought in a large quantity.

Individual teachers rarely have the opportunity to purchase textbooks for their classes. Textbook selections are not made every year and are often made by administrators or committees, instead of by individual classroom teachers. As a result, teachers often are faced with using a text that may not be easily understood by their students. When presented with such a challenge, teachers have two basic alternatives: to bypass the text and use other learning materials, or to guide students so they may learn from the required text.

A popular technique for bypassing the textbook is to lecture so thoroughly that students do not have to read the book. Even in your career as a successful student, you may have said something similar to, "I don't have to read the book. The teacher will tell me everything I need to know for the test." Videotapes, films, computers, and filmstrips can be used to present information. Of course, the obvious disadvantage of these approaches is that they do not give students opportunities to improve their reading so they might develop into independent readers.

It is occasionally possible for teachers to locate other textbooks or trade books written at lower levels of difficulty that present the content that is to be learned, although this solution is rarely practical given the limited financial resources and time that teachers have to prepare a lesson.

Teachers most often choose to provide sufficient guidance so students may learn from the required text.   This occurs because of the limited financial resources and time that were mentioned in the previous paragraph which prevent teachers from selecting alternative learning materials.   It also occurs because the prescribed textbook normally matches the school district's curriculum more closely than any other text.   Finally, some texts do not have convenient substitutes.   You cannot teach Dickens' A Tale of Two Cities, Hitler's Mein Kampf, or Kuhn's The Structure of Scientific Revolutions by reading other books.

How do teachers provide the guidance necessary for understanding materials that are too difficult for students to read and understand on their own? As you read in chapter #4, teachers can construct outlines, summaries, and structured arrays to present to students before they read to give them an overview of the information that will appear in the text.   This builds background and gives students a perspective from which to view the ideas in the text.

A second technique is to construct a reading guide.   Reading guides allow teachers to share their thoughts with students as students study, to think-along with students.   A reading guide normally contains an introduction that briefly describes what is to be learned, how the information relates to previous study, and why it is important to learn the new information.   The body of the guide directs students to important details and suggests approaches for reading the text. Commands and questions such as, "Name the three adjustment screws on the carburetor described on pages 543-556." and "What is the function of the butterfly valve?" direct students to information that teachers want them to learn. Recommendations such as "Reread the definition of torque in the chapter #3 before reading the section about transmissions in chapter #4.   Don't read the experiment described on pages 135-139 if you already understand that oil and water don't mix." and "It might help you to understand chapter #12 if you draw an analogy between voltage and water pressure." suggest ways of reading and thinking.   Effective teachers are good at predicting where students will encounter problems with learning and can offer suggestions in reading guides to help students overcome these obstacles.

A third technique for helping students understand a required text is to give them a simplified version of the text to read.   Teachers can rewrite paragraphs, chapters, or entire textbooks.   When rewriting, teachers try to eliminate unnecessary information, add concrete examples to explain abstract terms, add important detail, reorganize, simplify vocabulary, and shorten sentence length without creating confusion about the relationships among ideas.   For example, "Tom was happy.   Bill washed the car." is a shortened version of the original sentence, "Tom was happy, because Bill washed the car."   Unfortunately, the explicitness of the causal relationship is slightly muddied in the revised version, since other possibilities can be inferred when the logical connective "because" does not appear. By examining the two short sentences alone, we could infer that Tom was happy for a reason that was unrelated to the washing of the car. Tom might have been happy because he just bought a new electric train. Tom may not even know Bill.

There are disadvantages associated with the technique of rewriting required texts. First, rewriting takes a large amount of time. A teacher may spend 30 minutes or more on a 100-word passage. Second, it takes precious time and money to duplicate copies of the rewritten passages. Third, it may not be possible to simplify the information enough so that every student in the class can process the material, given that the range of secondary students' reading abilities may be eight years or more. Fourth, publishers may raise questions of plagiarism and copyright violation. Fifth, it is unethical to rewrite literature. Rewriting abuses an author, even on the rare occasion when the rewritten version is an improvement. Besides, the resulting product would be an abomination, not the author's book. For example, a colloquial version of Shakespeare's Romeo and Juliet was written a few years ago. The famous balcony scene included the following line: "Romeo, Romeo, where you at, man?" Certainly something was lost in the rewriting!

Choosing Procedures

The fourth step in planning is to decide which procedures to use when the lesson plan is implemented. Procedures are the methods that are used in conjunction with the facilities and materials to accomplish the goals. Choosing effective procedures is an important part of teaching.

There are numerous procedures for teaching. Teachers may decide to work with individuals, small groups, or large groups. Teachers may allow students to work without teacher intervention as individuals or in groups with their peers. Lectures, discussions, demonstrations, practices, panels, and debates may be used.

Effective teachers usually begin a new lesson by stating the goals and the importance of achieving them. This informs and motivates students. During the rest of the lesson, teachers use procedures that build prerequisite understandings, introduce the new content, offer guidance for learning, and provide sufficient feedback to student responses so that students are praised for effort and success and are given helpful suggestions for overcoming learning difficulty.

Formulating a Measurement and Evaluation Plan

The final step in lesson planning requires that teachers formulate a measurement and evaluation plan. Measurement is the process of determining amount or quantity. Evaluation is the process that examines measurement results and assigns a value to them. Evaluations indicate the worth of the results. When you step on a bathroom scale, you are measuring your weight. When you examine the result and decide that you are underweight, overweight, or at the ideal weight, you are evaluating.

A measurement and evaluation plan must be developed for deciding how and when to determine if the original goals were met by students. A good measurement and evaluation plan also requires that teachers be willing to identify reasons if a lesson is unsuccessful, and to decide whether teaching the content a second time is necessary.

When student performance is being measured, overt actions must be seen. For example, if a teacher wants to determine if a student can complete ten pushups in ten seconds, then the teacher will observe the student as the pushups are attempted. Covert actions such as "understanding" must be made operational. For example, understanding may be measured if a teacher defines it as correctly answering 90 percent of the questions about a reading passage in writing, or accurately spelling all ten of the key vocabulary words aloud.

Procedural and mechanical tasks, such as those commonly found in driver education, physical education, industrial education, drama classes, and music classes can be measured directly. Cognitive knowledge, however, is covert and cannot be measured directly. Teachers are forced to examine products of the mind which are related to cognitive knowledge, because they cannot directly observe the mental processes which create the product. As a result, teachers have traditionally relied on particular types of test items to encourage students to produce an observable product which reflected cognitive knowledge. We will describe two types of test items: those that require a student to supply the answer, and those that require a student to select the answer from a set of alternatives.

Essay and short-answer items are examples of test items that ask students to supply answers. Essay questions demand that students solve complex problems in written responses that range in length from a paragraph to a few pages. Short-answer items require students to add terms to incomplete sentences, or to write brief responses in one or two sentences. True-false, multiple choice, and matching items are examples of test items that ask students to choose from alternatives. Many teachers try to benefit from supply and select items by using both types on an examination.

Some experts prefer supply items to items where alternatives are provided, since they believe that supply items demand that students be more familiar with the content in question. Another advantage is that essay and short-answer items can be written relatively quickly when compared with tests that contain select items.

Difficulties arise, however, when the answers are examined. First, it usually takes longer to grade tests with supply items than tests with select items. Second, essay items sample content knowledge at a broader level than short-answer or select items. As a result, student scores may be misleading. It often happens that students have learned a lot that may not be measured by a test. In other frequent cases, students correctly predict the items that will appear on an examination, prepare on a limited basis, and are rewarded when the test fortuitously measures the little knowledge that they bring to the exam. Third, subjectivity and bias influence tests with supply items more than tests with select items. Since essay and short-answer items tend to ask for more divergent answers than convergent answers, the answers are inherently open to interpretation. In addition, bias creeps into scores on tests with supply items when teachers are subtly influenced by penmanship, neatness, spelling, or the personal relationship between the teacher and the student.

Suggestions for Writing and Grading Tests

Essay and Short-Answer Tests
1. Carefully choose verbs (ex., "compare, contrast, justify, define, evaluate, list") and be sure that students understand the meanings of the terms.
2. Specify required information. (ex., "Describe <u>five</u> economic advantages which favor capitalism over communism.")
3. Allow sufficient time so that the slower students are not rushed.
4. Write a model answer for each item to guide yourself in grading students' answers.
5. Evaluate tests before you identify the author. Grading anonymous papers will help you to be objective.
6. When grading papers, concentrate on the quality of the ideas expressed, rather than on style and mechanics. When students are given severe time

restrictions, they have little opportunity to revise and edit their answers.
7.   Feedback to students should always contain sincere, positive comments. Students will develop a dislike for tests, if they only receive criticism.

Multiple-Choice Tests
1.   The stem (the beginning of the item) should clearly state a meaningful problem.
2.   The distractors (incorrect alternative responses) should be plausible, so that the correct answer will be chosen only by students who truly understand the information.
3.   The number of distractors may be changed from item to item.
4.   The location of the correct response should vary from item to item. Careless test writers tend to locate correct responses in a particular place. For example, some authors favor the c location when they place the correct alternative.
5.   All distractors for an item should be the same approximate length. Often, test writers tend to make the correct alternative longer than the rest.
6.   Students should be allowed to see the test, their answers, and information identifying correct responses after the test is graded.

Measurement and evaluation are important so teachers can assess progress. Measurement and evaluation enable teachers to decide if the objectives for learning were met. This determination, however, does not represent the end of instructional decision making. It is part of a cycle. After determining what has been learned, teachers use that information to decide what will be learned in future lessons. The end of a lesson is also the beginning of a future lesson. The final evaluation provides the diagnostic information which serves as the foundation for future instructional decisions.

Teaching a Primary Generalization

1.   *Obtain diagnostic information*

Suppose that students only list pens, pencils, and chalk when asked to identify writing instruments. The teacher decides to broaden their understanding of the concept of writing instrument.

2.   *Establish goals*

Perhaps the teacher decides that every student should be able to write the generalization which states that all computerized word processors are writing instruments.

3.   *Select facilities and materials*

A good location for a lesson concerning computerized word processors would be the computer laboratory within a school. The teacher might take a pencil, pen, piece of chalk, paint brush, typewriter, letter stencil, bottle of ink, and a textbook to the laboratory. Computerized word processors and computers with word processing programs will be found in the laboratory. The students may not need to take any materials with them.

4.   *Choose procedures*

The procedures that are described below comprise a strategy that is effective when teaching primary generalizations.

a.   **The teacher states the goal and the importance of achieving it.**

In this case, the teacher may decide to say, "Today, we will see that computerized word processors can be categorized as writing instruments. This generalization will be important to us next week when we discuss the relative merits of various writing instruments."

b.   **The teacher presents examples of the key concept and asks students to discuss the similarities and differences among the examples. The quality of the feedback which the teacher and the students offer in response to a classmate's contribution is crucial.**

The teacher would show the pencil, pen, piece of chalk, paint brush, and typewriter to the class and ask them to discuss similarities and differences. The specific course of the discussion will depend on the teacher and students involved. However, students would probably note that the examples are similar in that they are commonly found in schools. Students would probably note that a pen and a typewriter make marks with ink, a pencil marks with lead, chalk marks with minerals, and brushes mark with paint. Students would probably note that pens, pencils, and typewriters mark on stationery, whereas chalk marks on slate and paint brushes mark on canvas and signs. Students would probably note that pencils, pens, pieces of chalk, and paint brushes are held in a person's hand, whereas the keys of a typewriter are pushed by hand.

c.   The teacher asks students to identify the most important common characteristics of the examples. The teacher asks students to name other examples that share the important common characteristic.

Students should be able to note that all of the examples are instruments that can be used to print letters, numbers, and symbols for the purpose of communicating.   Students might name scribes and typesetting machines as additional examples.

d.   The teacher presents the nonexamples and asks students to determine if they are examples of the category that accounts for the common characteristic that the previous examples shared.

When shown the letter stencil, bottle of ink, and textbook, and asked whether they should be categorized as writing instruments, students should be able to note the critical features which prevent the nonexamples from being placed in the category. Students would probably note that stencils and ink are not mechanical implements that can make letters, numbers, or symbols by themselves. They must be used in combination with marking instruments. Students would probably note that a book contains letters, numbers, and symbols but does not make them.

e.   The teacher asks the students to define the category they have been discussing.

The students might define a writing instrument as a self-contained tool that can be manipulated to print letters, numbers, and symbols for the purpose of communicating.

f.   The teacher presents the unfamiliar example and asks students whether it belongs to the category they have been discussing.

The teacher would demonstrate that a computerized word processor can be used to print messages on a monitor or on paper. When asked, students should be able to explain why they consider the computerized word processor to be an example of a writing instrument.

g.   Additional instances of the unfamiliar example are examined and the students are asked to prove a generalization through argument.

The teacher may demonstrate how each computerized word

processor in the laboratory works, or the students may be allowed to operate the machines by themselves. After their experiences with the machines, students should be able to argue, "If every computerized word processor encountered was a writing instrument, then all computerized word processors are writing instruments." In the experiences of these students, no exception to the generalization was found.

5. *Formulate a measurement and evaluation plan*

In this case, the teacher may have decided to have the students write the applicable generalization on a test the day after the lesson. If every student writes the correct answer, the lesson will be considered successful. If few students write the correct answer, the lesson will be considered a failure. The teacher will then carefully analyze what went wrong and will teach a similar lesson with appropriate improvements to all or some of the students.

Teaching a Hypothesis

1. *Obtain diagnostic information*

A teacher noticed that students tremendously enjoyed a social studies unit that dealt with advertising and marketing techniques. Students expressed a desire to study additional marketing campaigns. As a result, the teacher decides to enrich the backgrounds of students by presenting a lesson on a subject that is of interest to them.

2. *Establish goals*

The teacher decides that the group would benefit from a guided discussion that examines the evidence that supports rival hypotheses. Specifically, the class will discuss whether the decision to reformulate Coke was a debacle or a planned marketing strategy.

3. *Select facilities and materials*

The teacher decides to hold the discussion in the regular classroom. The teacher decides that chalk and a blackboard will be needed for the instructor, and two dittoed essays will be needed for each student. The teacher writes and duplicates the following essays.

a. **Coca-Cola Produces an Edsel**

The classic case of a marketing blunder was made by the Ford Motor Company when it introduced the Edsel in 1957. The car had some interesting features, such as an automatic transmission with push-button controls, and self-adjusting brakes. It also had an ugly name, an ugly grill, a powerful engine, and a high price. Ford did extensive research before the car came out, but consumer tastes changed in the interim. By 1957, people wanted inexpensive, smaller cars with less horsepower, like the Volkswagen Beetle, which was just being introduced to the American market. Ford dropped the Edsel from its line by 1959.

Recently, Coca-Cola made a similar mistake. Coke, which was the dominant soft drink for almost 100 years, began losing its share of the market in the 1970's to Pepsi. After several largely ineffectual counters, including comedian Bill Cosby's ridiculing of Pepsi's taste as too sweet, Coca-Cola introduced a new, sweeter formula to replace their original.

Coca-Cola had conducted more than 200,000 taste tests, which showed that 55% of those who were surveyed chose the new product. Fifty-five percent only indicates a slight preference, even when other things are equal. However, all other things weren't equal. A taste test is an artificial situation. Considerable scientific investigation has shown that most people cannot distinguish by taste alone from among American brands of colas, beers, bourbons, coffee, or cigarettes. Indeed, Gay Mullins, founder of the Old Cola drinkers, twice failed such a test on television.

Mullin's loyalty to the original Coke was undiminished, illustrating the danger of interpreting survey preference results as buying intentions. What consumers buy depends not only on taste preferences, but also on brand image, price, availability at stores and fountains, comments of friends, expected usage, cancer research reports, and the marketing strategies of competitors.

Predicting purchase patterns from survey data is not a perfect science. Specifically, in this case, one major error appears to have been in not telling respondents that their answers could result in the demise of the original formula. This was not the first time that marketing research was wrong.

Moreover, the consumer-manipulation theory requires that complex corporate plans for syrup manufacturing, distribution, and advertising be developed and coordinated over several months without leaks to the press. Certainly, someone at Coca-Cola who knew about such a story would sooner or later leak it.

b.   **Coca-Cola Displays Marketing Genius**

The people who developed the current marketing strategy for Coca-Cola deserve million-dollar bonuses for skillfully manipulating American consumers.

Coca-Cola felt that its century-old drink was being taken for granted. Something had to be done to spark interest in the product. As a result, Coca-Cola decided to introduce a new version of its cola, threaten to eliminate its classic beverage, wait for the public outcry, then to magnanimously return the original as if the company were being responsive to consumer pressure.

At company headquarters in Atlanta, executives must have paid rapt attention as their marketing strategists gleefully emphasized the numerous advantages to their plan. First, Coca-Cola would have a sweeter drink that would compete better with Pepsi. Second, the company would not ultimately lose its satisfied customers, since it would retain the original drink. Third, Coca-Cola would have two strong brands to stock in supermarkets, thus squeezing smaller cola manufacturers off the shelves and reducing competition. Fourth, the value of old promotional items and reproductions, such as bottle openers, trays, and signs would increase. Fifth, grassroots consumer revolutions would draw the attention of the international media, resulting in massive, free publicity for the company. Sixth, the company would be praised for its concern for consumers, after it announced that it was returning the old version to the market.

On April 23, 1985, Coca-Cola put its plan into action and watched all of its expectations come true. Consumers rushed to buy the remaining cans of old Coke, the novel new Coke, and souvenirs. Consumers clamored for the return of their favorite drink. Even President Reagan confessed that he and Nancy found the new Coke "a little wimpy" and that they were hoarding 26 cases of the old Coke in the galley of Air Force One.

On July 10, 1985, the president of Coca-Cola solemnly announced the return of Coca-Cola Classic. Marketing Strategists were probably taking well-earned vacations in Tahiti.

4.   *Choose procedures*

a.   **The teacher states the goals of the lesson and the importance of achieving them.**

The teacher may plan to say, "Today, we will examine two hypotheses which explain the actions of the Coca-Cola Company when it eliminated, then returned, its classic beverage. Our lesson will broaden your understanding of marketing techniques and will give you practice in analyzing arguments."

b.   **Students are given a purpose for completing the first activity.**

The teacher distributes the passage entitled "Coca-Cola Produces an Edsel" and tells students that they will have ample time to silently read the essay for the purpose of identifying the hypothesis and the three pieces of evidence which support it.

c.   **After completing the activity, the teacher asks the students to state the hypothesis and to decide if it is plausible.**

A student might accurately state, "The hypothesis is that the Coca-Cola Company blundered when it decided to take its classic beverage off the market. The hypothesis is plausible."

The teacher then writes the hypothesis on the blackboard.

d.   **The teacher asks questions and provides appropriate feedback to lead students to the identification of the evidence.**

As students correctly identify each of the three pieces of evidence, the teacher writes it on the blackboard.

e.   **The teacher asks students to judge the validity, reliability, and relevance of each piece of information and the overall impressiveness of the evidence.**

Students might indicate that one piece of evidence is that the company overestimated the importance of the results of the taste tests. A large sample was tested, but the percentage of people who preferred the new Coke to the old Coke was not high. Almost as many people preferred the old Coke. In addition, the results of taste tests are not very reliable. Finally, a major flaw in the tests was that respondents were not told that their answers could result in the demise of the original drink.

Students might indicate that a second piece of evidence suggesting that the company blundered is that it did not investigate other critical variables which influence buying, such as image, price, availability, and the recommendations of friends.

Students might mention the third piece of evidence. If the company had intentionally planned to dupe consumers, word of the plan would have probably leaked from company sources. No pertinent leaks appeared.

Students may determine that the evidence suggests that the company made a mistake. The evidence is relevant. Additionally, the weight of the evidence is convincing.

f.   **The teacher asks the students to put the argument proving the hypothesis in "If...,then..." form.**

A student would say, "If the significance of the taste tests was overestimated, additional important variables were never investigated, and no leaks regarding the manipulation of consumers developed, then the Coca-Cola Company blundered when it decided to take its classic beverage off the market."

g.   **Students are given a purpose for completing the second activity.**

The teacher distributes the passage entitled "Coca-Cola Displays Marketing Genius" and tells students that they will have ample time to silently read the essay for the purpose of identifying the second hypothesis and the six pieces of evidence which support it.

h.   **After completing the activity, the teacher asks the students to state the hypothesis and to decide if it is plausible.**

A student might accurately state, "The hypothesis is that the Coca-Cola Company deliberately planned to manipulate consumers. The hypothesis is plausible."

The teacher then writes the hypothesis on the blackboard.

i.   **The teacher asks questions and provides appropriate feedback to lead students to the identification of the evidence.**

As students correctly identify each of the six pieces of evidence, the teacher writes it on the blackboard.

j.   **The teacher asks the students to judge the validity and relevance of each piece of information and the overall impressiveness of the evidence.**

Students might indicate that one piece of evidence is that the company ultimately gained new customers by offering a flavor that was similar to the taste of Pepsi.

A second piece of evidence is that old customers were retained, since the original flavor of Coke was still offered.

A third piece of evidence is that sales of merchandise with the company's logos increased.

A fourth piece of evidence is that there was less shelf space for colas manufactured by less popular companies.

A fifth piece of evidence is that the company received a great deal of attention from the media at no cost.

Finally, students might indicate that Coca-Cola did present itself in a favorable light by announcing that their reintroduction of the classic Coke was a sign of their overwhelming concern for consumers. The company presented itself as being forthright and responsive.

Students may determine that the evidence is relevant and convincing.

k.   **The teacher asks the students to put the argument proving the hypothesis in "If..., then..." form.**

A student would say, "If the company predicted that it would gain new customers, retain old customers, increase the sales of promotional items, force other manufacturers from store shelves, receive extensive free publicity, and leave the impression of being responsive to the desires of consumers, then the Coca-Cola Company deliberately planned to manipulate consumers."

l.   **The teacher asks if there is additional evidence to support either hypothesis that the students would like to have.**

A student might say, "It would be nice if we could ask the

company what they intended."

The teacher might respond, "In fact, when asked if the company had originally planned to manipulate consumers, Donald Keough, president of Coca-Cola, replied, 'The truth is we're not that dumb and we're not that smart.' Believe it, or not!"

m.   **The teacher asks if the students can think of other attractive hypotheses.**

n.   **The teacher closes the lesson by asking students to indicate which hypothesis they prefer.**

The teacher may ask the students to raise their hands to show their preferences. A tally is not taken, since the teacher does not want to give the impression that truth is decided by vote.

5.   *Formulate a measurement and evaluation plan*

The teacher decides to evaluate immediately after the lesson. The teacher decides to consider the lesson a success if students are enthusiastic, participate, identify all critical evidence, state the two rival hypotheses, and express a preference.

Teaching an Evaluation

1.   *Obtain diagnostic information*

A biology teacher is preparing to have students read a chapter from a textbook which explains that certain animals are used in research studies because of the physiological similarities between them and humans. The teacher knows from past experience that students are often shocked when they read about the treatments that some animals receive. As a result, discussions have focused more on the desirability of using animals in experiments, rather than on physiology. The teacher decides that it would be better to treat the two important issues fully and separately. The teacher decides to discuss the issue of desirability before the textbook is read, so that students can concentrate on the physiological similarities when the text is read.

2.   *Establish goals*

For the first part of the lesson, the teacher hopes to help students identify the evaluations they hold regarding the use of animals in experiments and the evidence that they use to support their evaluations.

3.   *Select facilities and materials*

The teacher decides to use the regular classroom.

The teacher chooses provocative material and writes questions for the students to answer. A sheet containing the passage and the questions is duplicated for each student. An example is given below.

a.   P.E.T.A., People for the Ethical Treatment of Animals, is a nonprofit organization which objects to the cruel treatment of laboratory animals. Dogs, rabbits, monkeys, cats, guinea pigs, and mice are often subjected to barbaric treatments when they are used to test cosmetics, chemicals, and medicines.

For example, animals are forced to drink drain cleaner, which causes convulsions, paralysis, and bleeding.

Another test measures the irritancy of products that might get into a person's eyes. Rabbits are placed in stocks to prevent them from clawing their eyes to dislodge the irritating substance. Only their necks and heads protrude. The lower lid of the rabbit's eye is pulled away from the eyeball to form a small cup. Into that cup is dropped some of the substance to be tested. The eye is then held closed for several seconds while the animal screams in pain. The other eye is left untreated to serve as a control. The rabbit's eyes are then observed at specific intervals to see how severe the irritation is, or if blindness is caused.

Even more distressing, is the practice of vivisection. Vivisection is the act of cutting into or dissecting a living animal, especially for scientific research. The late George Bernard Shaw said, "You do not settle whether an experiment is justified or not by merely showing that it is of some use. The distinction is not between useful and useless experiments, but between barbarous and civilized behavior. Vivisection is a social evil because if it advances human knowledge, it does so at the expense of human character."

If you are interested in the work that is done by P.E.T.A. to prevent cruel treatment of laboratory animals, you can write the organization at Box 42516, Washington, D.C., 20015, for more information.

Questions

1.   What evidence is given in the article which supports the evaluation that animals should not be treated cruelly in experiments? State the argument, the evidence, and evaluation in If..., then... form.

2.   Do you know of other cases where animals have been treated cruelly in experiments?

3.   What virtues would be satisfied if animals were treated kindly?

4.   Can you think of a position that falls on a continuum somewhere between the extremes of not using animals at all and treating animals cruelly in experiments?

5.   What virtues would be satisfied by the position you identified in question #4?

6.   What position regarding the use of animals in experiments do you prefer?

4.   *Choose procedures*

a.   **The teacher states the goal and the importance of achieving it.**

The teacher might say, "We are going to begin the next unit by examining whether animals should be treated cruelly in experiments. This interesting issue should be considered so that you can clearly focus on the physiological similarities between people and the animals that are frequently used as subjects in research experiments when you read the next chapter in your textbook."

b.   **The teacher distributes the instructional materials and explains the work that is required.**

In this case, the teacher might say, "Before class tomorrow, please read the article concerning People for the Ethical Treatment of Animals and answer the attached questions in writing. Put your student identification number on your answer sheet, instead of your name. Tomorrow, your papers will be read by your peers. Interesting answers will be read aloud to the entire class. Finally, I will collect the papers and assign grades based on content and mechanics. Any position that you take is acceptable. Your content grade will depend on the clarity of your presentation."

Alternative approaches can be used. However, this procedure assures anonymity, which is important so that students do not directly expose themselves to ridicule when their peers read their honest, highly personal evaluations. This procedure also allows ample time for reflection, encourages students to express themselves clearly by committing their thoughts to print, informs students of their audiences, describes the activities in the lesson, and informs students of the grading criteria. Most importantly, this procedure requires that each student fully respond. Every student is convinced that their thinking and participation matter. Students are not allowed to sit passively, nor will a few students be able to dominate the discussion and/or force their views on others. The teacher is ensuring that all views will be presented. The teacher shows students that they are ultimately responsible for the choices they make in their lives. Reaching group consensus should not be the ultimate goal when evaluations are discussed.

c.   **The classroom activities are initiated on the proceeding day.**

The teacher decides to collect the coded papers, shuffle them, distribute them, and ask to be sure that students do not receive their own papers.

d.   **The class identifies the evaluation(s) and evidence in question. The students state the argument(s) in "If..., then..." form.**

The teacher decides to have the students read the responses to question 1 that appear on the papers in front of them. In this case, question 1 asked students to identify the evaluation, evidence, and argument in the assigned article. After reading the responses from their peers, students are asked to raise their hands if they think they have a good answer to share with the class. If the teacher does not get a satisfactory answer from the first student who responds, feedback will be encouraged as other students will be asked to complete the answer.

Students should be able to identify the evaluation that animals should not be treated cruelly. The evidence is that animals are tortured and that people act inhumanely when they brutalize animals. The argument is, "If animals are tortured and people act inhumanely when they brutalize animals, then animals used in experiments should not be treated cruelly."

e.   **The class shares other cases that support the evaluation.**

Question 2 asks students to delve into their backgrounds of knowledge to recall similar instances of cruelty to research animals. Students might mention experiments where animals were given inordinate amounts of caffeine, nicotine, or saccharine in an effort to induce cancer.

f.   **The class identifies additional virtues that would be satisfied by the evaluation.**

The students silently read and then share responses to question 3. In addition to the personal satisfaction of acting compassionately (personal truth) and the satisfaction of having other people act nobly (social justice), which are mentioned in the article, students may say that virtues related to aesthetic beauty and religious justice are addressed. If people did not maim or disfigure animals, then the natural beauty of animals would be preserved. If people did not tamper with nature, then their actions would be consistent with the religious view that a sin against nature would be a sin against a transcendental power.

g.   **The class identifies positions that fall on a continuum between the evaluation and its opposite.**

Students would share their answers to question 4. The greatest compassion would be shown if animals were not involved in research experiments at all. The opposite of treating animals kindly is to treat them cruelly. The obvious, moderate position would be to treat animals as kindly as possible whenever they have to be used in crucial experiments.

h.   **The class describes the virtues that would be satisfied by each moderate position.**

Question 5 addresses this issue. A student might say, "I would feel more compassionate if I treated or caused others to treat animals more kindly. If harm to animals were minimized, there would be less damage to their natural health and beauty. Other people would feel better about themselves if they treated animals as kindly as possible. Successful, significant experiments could contribute to the knowledge and health of human and animal societies. Finally, eventual contributions to the health of animals and people would probably be pleasing to a transcendental power."

i.   **Students may be asked to identify the evaluations they prefer.**

This final step adds closure to the lesson. In this case, question 6 encourages students to make a choice. As with hypotheses, no tally of preferences is taken so that students are not led to think that the majority, or consensus, view is the best.

When dealing with highly sensitive or controversial issues, the teacher may not wish to have students identify their preferences. In such cases, closure can be provided if the teacher asks students to think about their individual preferences, or to summarize the arguments that were discussed during the lesson.

5.   *Formulate a measurement and evaluation plan*

The teacher decides to evaluate the effectiveness of the lesson for the group and for individuals. First, the teacher will consider the lesson to be successful if students are enthusiastic, participate, and if the group discussion results in the identification of alternative evaluations and the evidence which supports them. In addition to observational evidence, the teacher will ask students on the day after the lesson to write a paragraph critiquing the lesson and describing their reactions to it. Second, the teacher will evaluate the effectiveness of the lesson for individuals when grading each student's answers to the questions in the lesson.

Conclusion

We hope that this chapter has convinced you that teaching is a decision-making process that helps teachers make sense of instructional tasks. Teachers adopt a general instructional strategy and specific strategies for obtaining diagnostic information, establishing goals, selecting facilities and materials, choosing procedures, and formulating a plan for measurement and evaluation.

We also hope that the sample lesson plans showed you some techniques that you may wish to apply in your own classrooms. The techniques that were described are not the only ones which can be used to teach generalizations, hypotheses, or evaluations. However, every lesson should include a conclusion, evidence which supports the conclusion, and a statement of the argument which joins the evidence and the conclusion. Deciding on the appropriateness of evidence depends on the type of conclusion under consideration. A generalization is supported by repeated instances. A hypothesis is supported by evidence from a variety of sources. An evaluation is supported by subjective standards of judgement.

Index

Alienation 46
Anxiety 37, 99
    reducing 99
Argument
    by agreement 18
    by difference 18
    by variation 18
    from convenience 24
    from instances 16
    probable 17
Assertion 6
Audience 75
Auditory disturbances 35
Authorities 13
Background knowledge 38, 71, 91
Beauty 22
Cause 18, 19
Conventions 72
Creative writing 75
Curriculum guide 115
Definition 7, 8
    accidental 9
    adequate 7
    causal 9
    distinctive 8
    etymological 8
    genetic 8
    ideal 7
    nominal 8
    synonymous 8
    translation 8
Emotion 22, 37, 39, 69, 70, 76
Evaluation 6, 21, 122
    examples 24, 62, 83
    formation 22
    standards of 22
    weighing 26
Evidence
    probability 17

    relevancy 17
    reliability 17
    sufficiency 17
    validity 17
Fact and opinion 6
Feedback 78, 94, 96
Generalization 6, 10
    examples 10, 58
    formation 12
    functional 9
    primary 7
    statistical 9
Hypothesis 6, 16
    alternative 17
    causal 18
    examples 19, 60
Instructional adjustments
    alternative resources 119
    bypassing the text 119
    guidance 119, 120
    rewriting text 120
Interviews 110
Justice
    religious 23
    social 23
Language and thought 26
Lesson plans 14
Library research 105
    almanacs 106
    articles 109
    atlases 106
    books of quotations 106
    card catalog 107
    dictionaries 106
    encyclopedias 106
    reference books 106, 107
Magazines 43
Measurement 122
Memory 28, 40, 71, 85, 97, 99
Metacognition 14, 49, 81
Mnemonic devices 96

keyword technique 98
loci method 97
pegword technique 97
Morphology 38
Newspapers 43
Notes 95
Orthography 38, 73
Outlining 93
Phonology 38
Print 66
Purpose 35, 69
entertainment 35, 69
information and guidance 35, 69
knowledge 35, 69
personal enjoyment 35, 69
personal improvement 35, 69
pleasure 35, 69
Readability
cloze technique 118
formulas 117
reading inventory 118
Reading
and evaluations 62
and generalizations 51, 58
and hypotheses 60
and language 41
definition of 48, 50
standardized tests 117
Reading Rate
influences 90
mechanical training 92
potential speed 91
scanning 90
skimming 90
Register 75, 76
Rhetorical Patterns 39, 43, 73
Sampling
enumeration 14
random 15
stratified random 15
time-lapse 15

Scientific method 14
Self-esteem 37, 70
Semantics 39, 73
Sentence 83
Standard problem solving technique 14, 115
Structural generalizations 53
Structured array 95
Study strategies
      EVOKER 89
      SQ3R 89
      SQRQCQ 89
Summary 94
Syntax 39, 73
Teachers 45, 47
Teaching
      a hypothesis 127
      a primary generalization 124
      an evaluation 133
Test items 122
Test-wiseness 104
Textbooks 42
Time management 111
Truth
      evidential 22
      personal 22
Typography 38, 53, 73, 85
Underlining 93
Understanding 63
Visual disturbances 35
Word 57
Writing
      and evaluations 82
      and generalizations 82
      and hypotheses 82
      definition of 80, 82
      environment 76
      feedback 78
      tools 72
      visual appearance 74